Language and gender: making the difference

Cate Poynton

Series Editor: Frances Christie

Oxford University Press
1989

Oxford University Press
Walton Street, Oxford OX2 6DP

Oxford   New York   Toronto
Delhi   Bombay   Calcutta   Madras   Karachi
Petaling Jaya   Singapore   Hong Kong   Tokyo
Nairobi   Dar es Salaam   Cape Town
Melbourne   Auckland

and associated companies in
Berlin   Ibadan

Oxford English and the *Oxford English* logo are trade marks of
Oxford University Press

ISBN 0 19 437160 3

© Deakin University 1985, 1989

First published 1985
Second edition 1989

Printed in Hong Kong.

About the author

Cate Poynton

Cate Poynton grew up in Melbourne and gradu-
ated from the University of Melbourne in
English Language and Literature. She became
a teacher, then got involved in teacher education, developing language studies courses
primarily for teachers of English as mother
tongue. The first meeting with linguistics
turned out to be quite addictive: she's still
hooked and currently completing a PhD at the
University of Sydney. Her thesis is on tenor
(negotiating relationships through language), looking particularly at
address forms. As well as being linguistically revealing, her data—
especially on insults!—has proved to have high entertainment value for
friends and colleagues alike. She lectures in Communication Studies at
the South Australian College of Advanced Education.

The limits of my language are the limits of my world.
Ludwig Wittgenstein

The grammar of a language is its theory of reality.
Gunther Kress and Robert Hodge

Power is the ability to impose one's definition of what is possible, what is right, what is rational, what is real.
Pamela Fishman

In a world where language and naming are power, silence is oppression, is violence.
Adrienne Rich

Special acknowledgement

Without the work, published and in progress, of all the members of the Register Working Group at the University of Sydney, in particular that of Jim Martin, and without the willingness of individual members of that group, in particular Joan Rothery, Guenter Plum, and Chris Nesbitt, to listen and help think through old and new ideas from the inchoate to the possibly useful stage, this work would not have been possible. My thanks to them all.

Foreword

In a sense, educational interest in language is not new. Studies of rhetoric and of grammar go back as far as the Greeks; in the English-speaking countries, studies of the classical languages, and more recently of English itself, have had a well established place in educational practice. Moreover, a number of the issues which have aroused the most passionate debates about how to develop language abilities have tended to remain, resurfacing at various points in history in somewhat different formulations perhaps, but nonetheless still there, and still lively.

Of these issues, probably the most lively has been that concerning the extent to which explicit knowledge about language on the part of the learner is a desirable or a useful thing. But the manner in which discussion about this issue has been conducted has often been allowed to obscure other and bigger questions: questions, for example, both about the nature of language as an aspect of human experience, and about language as a resource of fundamental importance in the building of human experience. The tendency in much of the western intellectual tradition has been to dissociate language and experience, in such a way that language is seen as rather neutral, merely serving to 'carry' the fruits of experience. Whereas in this view language is seen as a kind of 'conduit', subservient to experience in various ways, an alternative view, as propounded in the books in this series, would argue that language is itself not only a part of experience, but intimately involved in the manner in which we construct and organise experience. As such, it is never neutral, but deeply implicated in building meaning. One's notions concerning how to teach about language will differ quite markedly, depending upon the view one adopts concerning language and experience. In fact, though discussions concerning teaching about language can sometimes be interesting, in practice many such discussions have proved theoretically ill-founded and barren, serving merely to perpetuate a number of unhelpful myths about language.

The most serious and confusing of these myths are those which would suggest we can dissociate language from meaning — form from function, or form from 'content'. Where such myths apply, teaching about language becomes a matter of teaching about 'language rules' — normally grammatical rules — and as history has demonstrated over the years, such teaching rapidly degenerates into the arid pursuit of parts of speech and the parsing of isolated sentences. Meaning, and the critical role of language in the building of meaning, are simply overlooked, and the kinds of knowledge about language made available to the learner are of a very limited kind.

The volumes in this series of monographs devoted to language education in my view provide a much better basis upon which to address questions related to the teaching about language than has been the case anywhere in the English-speaking world for some time now. I make this claim for several reasons, one of the most important being that the series never sought directly to establish a model for teaching about language at all. On the contrary, it sought to establish a principled model of language, which, once properly articulated, allows us to address many questions of an educational nature, including those to do with teaching about language. To use Halliday's term (1978), such a model sees language primarily as a 'social semiotic', and as a resource for meaning, centrally involved in the processes by which human beings negotiate, construct and change the nature of social experience. While the series certainly does not claim to have had the last word on these and related subjects, I believe it does do much to set a new educational agenda — one which enables us to look closely at the role of language both in living and in learning: one which, moreover, provides a basis upon which to decide those kinds of teaching and learning about language which may make a legitimate contribution to the development of the learner.

I have said that arguments to do with teaching about language have been around for a long time: certainly as long as the two hundred years of white settlement in Australia. In fact, coincidentally, just as the first settlers were taking up their enforced residence in the Australian colony of New South Wales, Lindley Murray was preparing his *English Grammar* (1795), which, though not the only volume produced on the subject in the eighteenth century, was certainly the best. Hundreds of school grammars that were to appear in Britain and Australia for the next century at least, were to draw very heavily upon what Murray had written. The parts of speech, parsing and sentence analysis, the latter as propounded by Morell (an influential inspector of schools in England), were the principal elements in the teaching about language in the Australian colonies, much as they were in England throughout the century. By the 1860s and 1870s the Professor of Classics and Logic at Sydney University, Charles Badham, who had arrived from England in 1867, publicly disagreed with the examining authorities in New South Wales concerning the teaching of grammar. To the contemporary reader there is a surprising modernity about many of his objections, most notably his strongly held conviction that successful control of one's language is learned less as a matter of committing to memory the parts of speech and the principles of parsing, than as a matter of frequent opportunity for use.

Historically, the study by which issues of use had been most effectively addressed had been that of rhetoric, in itself quite old in the English-speaking tradition, dating back at least to the sixteenth century. Rhetorical studies flourished in the eighteenth century, the best known works on the subject being George Campbell's *The Philosophy of Rhetoric* (1776), and Hugh Blair's *Lectures on Rhetoric and Belles Lettres* (1783), while in the nineteenth century Richard Whately published his work, *Elements of Rhetoric* (1828). As the nineteenth century proceeded, scholarly work on rhetoric declined, as was testified by the markedly inferior but nonetheless influential works of Alexander Bain (*English Composition and Rhetoric*, 1866; Revised version, 1887). Bain, in fact, did much to corrupt and destroy the older rhetorical traditions, primarily because he lost sight of the need for a basic concern with meaning in language. Bain's was the century of romanticism after all: on the one hand, Matthew Arnold was extolling the civilising influence of English literature in the development of children; on the other hand, there was a tendency towards suspicion, even contempt, for those who wanted to take a scholarly look at the linguistic organisation of texts, and at the ways in which they were structured for the building of meaning. In 1921, Ballard (who was an expert witness before the Newbolt Enquiry on the teaching of English), wrote a book called *Teaching the Mother Tongue*, in which he noted among other things, that unfortunately in England at least rhetorical studies had become associated with what were thought to be rather shallow devices for persuasion and argument. The disinclination to take seriously the study of the rhetorical organisation of texts gave rise to a surprisingly unhelpful tradition for the teaching of literature, which is with us yet in many places: 'civilising' it might be, but it was *not* to be the object of systematic study, for such study would in some ill-defined way threaten or devalue the work of literature itself.

A grammarian like Murray had never been in doubt about the relationship of grammar and rhetoric. As he examined it, grammar was concerned with the syntax of the written English sentence: it was not concerned with the study of 'style', about which he wrote a short appendix in his original grammar, where his debt to the major rhetoricians of the period was apparent. Rhetorical studies, especially as discussed by Campbell for instance, did address questions of 'style', always from the standpoint of a recognition of the close relationship of language to the socially created purpose in using language. In fact, the general model of language as discussed by Campbell bore some relationship to the model taken up in this series, most notably in its commitment to register.

The notion of register proposes a very intimate relationship of text to context: indeed, so intimate is that relationship, it is asserted, that the one can only be interpreted by reference to the other. Meaning is realised in language (in the form of text), which is thus shaped or patterned in response to the context of situation in which it is used. To study language then, is to concentrate upon exploring how it is systematically patterned towards important social ends. The linguistic theory adopted here is that of systemic linguistics. Such a linguistic theory is itself also a social theory, for it proposes firstly, that it is in the nature of human behaviour to build reality and/or experience through complex semiotic processes, and secondly, that the principal semiotic system available to humans is their language. In this sense, to study language is to explore some of the most important and pervasive of the processes by which human beings build their world.

I originally developed the volumes in this series as the basis of two major off campus courses in Language Education taught in the Master's degree program at Deakin University, Victoria, Australia. To the best of my knowledge, such courses, which are designed primarily for teachers and teacher educators, are the first of their kind in the world, and while they actually appeared in the mid 1980s, they emerge from work in language education which has been going on in Australia for some time. This included the national Language Development Project, to which Michael Halliday was consultant, and whose work I co-ordinated throughout its second, productive phase. (This major project was initiated by the Commonwealth Government's Curriculum Development Centre, Canberra, in the 1970s, and involved the co-operation of curriculum development teams from all Australian states in developing language curriculum materials. Its work was not completed because of political changes which caused the activities of the Curriculum Development Centre to be wound down.) In the 1980s a number of conferences have been held fairly regularly in different parts of Australia, all of them variously exploring aspects of language education, and leading to the publication of a number of conference reports. They include: Frances Christie (ed.), *Language and the Social Construction of Experience* (Deakin University, 1983); Brendan Bartlett and John Carr (eds.), *Language in Education Workshop: a Report of Proceedings* (Centre for Research and Learning, Brisbane C.A.E., Mount Gravatt Campus, Brisbane, 1984); Ruqaiya Hasan (ed.), *Discourse on Discourse* (Applied Linguistics Association of Australia, Occasional Papers, Number 7, 1985); Clare Painter and J.R. Martin (eds.), *Writing to Mean: Teaching Genres across the Curriculum* (Applied Linguistics Association of Australia, Occasional Papers, Number 9, 1986); Linda Gerot, Jane Oldenburg and Theo Van Leeuwen (eds.), *Language and Socialisation: Home and School* (in preparation). All these activities have contributed to the building of a climate of opinion and a tradition of thinking about language which made possible the development of the volumes in this series.

While it is true that the developing tradition of language education which these volumes represent does, as I have noted, take up some of the concerns of the older rhetorical studies, it nonetheless also looks forward, pointing to ways of examining language which were not available in earlier times. For example, the notion of language as a social semiotic, and its associated conception of experience or reality as socially built and constantly subject to processes of transformation, finds very much better expression today than would have been possible before, though obviously much more requires to be said about this than can be dealt with in these volumes. In addition, a functionally driven view of language is now available, currently most completely articulated in Halliday's *An Introduction to Functional Grammar* (1985), which offers ways of understanding the English language in a manner that Murray's Grammar could not have done.

Murray's Grammar confined itself to considerations of the syntax of the written English sentence. It did not have anything of use to say about spoken language, as opposed to written language, and, equally, it provided no basis upon which to explore a unit other than the sentence, whether that be the paragraph, or, even more importantly, the total text. The preoccupation with the written sentence reflected the pre-eminent position being accorded to the written word by Murray's time, leading to disastrous consequences since, that is the diminished value accorded to spoken language, especially in educational practices. In Murray's work, the lack of a direct relationship between the study of grammar on the one hand, and that of 'style', on the other hand, was, as I have already noted, to be attributed to his view that it was the rhetorician who addressed wider questions relating to the text. In the tradition in which he worked, in fact, grammar looked at syntactic rules divorced from considerations of meaning or social purpose.

By contrast, Halliday's approach to grammar has a number of real strengths, the first of which is the fact that its basis is semantic, not syntactic: that is to say, it is a semantically driven grammar, which, while not denying that certain principles of syntax do apply, seeks to consider and identify the role of various linguistic items in any text in terms of their function in building meaning. It is for this reason that its practices for interpreting and labelling various linguistic items and groupings are functionally based, not syntactically based. There is in other words, no dissociation of 'grammar' on the one hand and 'semantics' or meaning on the other. A second strength of Halliday's approach is that it is not uniquely interested in written language, being instead committed to the study of both the spoken and written modes, and to an explanation of the differences between the two, in such a way that each is illuminated because of its contrast with the other. A third and final strength of the systemic functional grammar is that it permits useful movement across the text, addressing the manner in which linguistic patternings are built up for the construction of the overall text in its particular 'genre', shaped as it is in response to the context of situation which gave rise to it.

Halliday's functional grammar lies behind all ten volumes in this series, though one other volume, by Michael Christie, called *Aboriginal perspectives on experience and learning: the role of language in Aboriginal Education*, draws upon somewhat different if still compatible perspectives in educational and language theory to develop its arguments. The latter volume, is available directly from Deakin University. In varying ways, the volumes in this series provide a helpful introduction to much that is more fully dealt with in Halliday's Grammar, and I commend the series to the reader who wants to develop some sense of the ways such a body of linguistic theory can be applied to educational questions. A version of the grammar specifically designed for teacher education remains to be written, and while I cherish ambitions to begin work on such a version soon, I am aware that others have similar ambitions — in itself a most desirable development.

While I have just suggested that the reader who picks up any of the volumes in this series should find ways to apply systemic linguistic theory to educational theory, I want to argue, however, that what is offered here is more than merely a course in applied linguistics, legitimate though such a course might be. Rather, I want to claim that this is a course in educational linguistics, a term of importance because it places linguistic study firmly at the heart of educational enquiry. While it is true that a great deal of linguistic research of the past, where it did not interpret language in terms of interactive, social processes, or where it was not grounded in a concern for meaning, has had little of relevance to offer education, socially relevant traditions of linguistics like that from which systemics is derived, do have a lot to contribute. How that contribution should be articulated is quite properly a matter of development in partnership between educationists, teachers and linguistics, and a great deal has yet to be done to achieve such articulation.

I believe that work in Australia currently is making a major contribution to the development of a vigorous educational linguistics, not all of it of course in a systemic framework. I would note here the important work of such people as J.R. Martin, Joan Rothery, Suzanne Eggins and Peter Wignell of the University of Sydney, investigating children's writing development; the innovatory work of Brian Gray and his colleagues a few years ago in developing language programs for Aboriginal children in central Australia, and more recently his work with other groups in Canberra; the recent work of Beth Graham, Michael Christie and Stephen Harris, all of the Northern Territory Department of Education, in developing language programs for Aboriginal children; the important work of John Carr and his colleagues of the Queensland Department of Education in developing new perspectives upon language in the various language curriculum guidelines they have prepared for their state; the contributions of Jenny Hammond of the University of Wollongong, New South Wales, in her research into language development in schools, as well as the various programs in which she teaches; research being undertaken by Ruqaiya Hasan and Carmel Cloran of Macquarie University, Sydney, into children's language learning styles in the transition years from home to school; investigations by Linda Gerot, also of Macquarie University, into classroom discourse in the secondary school, across a number of different subjects; and the work of Pam Gilbert of James Cook University, Townsville, in Queensland, whose interests are both in writing in the secondary school, and in language and gender.

The signs are that a coherent educational linguistics is beginning to appear around the world, and I note with pleasure the appearance of two new and valuable international journals: *Language and Education*, edited by David Corson of Massey University, New Zealand, and *Linguistics in Education*, edited by David Bloome, of the University of Massachusetts. Both are committed to the development of an educational linguistics, to which many traditions of study, linguistic, semiotic and sociological, will no doubt make an important contribution. Such an educational linguistics is long overdue, and in what are politically difficult times, I suggest such a study can make a major contribution to the pursuit of educational equality of opportunity, and to attacking the wider social problems of equity and justice. Language is a political institution: those who are wise in its ways, capable of using it to shape and serve important personal and social goals, will be the ones who are 'empowered' (to use a fashionable word): able, that is, not merely to participate effectively *in* the world, but able also *to act upon it*, in the sense that they can strive for significant social change. Looked at in these terms, provision of appropriate language education programs is a profoundly important matter, both in ensuring equality of educational opportunity, and in helping to develop those who are able and willing to take an effective role in democratic processes of all kinds.

One of the most encouraging measures of the potential value of the perspectives open to teachers taking up an educational linguistics of the kind offered in these monographs, has been the variety of teachers attracted to the courses of which they form a part, and the ways in which these teachers have used what they have learned in undertaking research papers for the award of the master's degree. They include, for example, secondary teachers of physics, social science, geography and English, specialists in teaching English as a second language to migrants and specialists in teaching English to Aboriginal people, primary school teachers, a nurse educator, teachers of illiterate adults, and language curriculum consultants, as well as a number of teacher educators with specialist responsibilities in teaching language education. For many of these people the perspectives offered by an educational linguistics are both new and challenging, causing them to review and change aspects of their teaching practices in various ways. Coming to terms with a semantically driven grammar is in itself quite demanding, while there is often considerable effort involved to bring to conscious awareness the ways in which we use language for the realisation of different meanings. But the effort is plainly worth it, principally because of the added sense of control and direction it can give teachers interested to work at fostering and developing students who are independent and confident in using language for the achievement of various goals. Those people for whom these books have proved helpful, tend to say that they have achieved a stronger and richer appreciation of language and how it works than they had before; that because they know considerably more about language themselves, they are able to intervene much more effectively in directing and guiding those whom they teach; that because they have a better sense of the relationship of language and 'content' than they had before, they can better guide their students into control of the 'content' of the various subjects for which they are responsible; and finally, that because they have an improved sense of how to direct language learning, they are able to institute new assessment policies, negotiating, defining and clarifying realistic goals for their students. By any standards, these are considerable achievements.

As I draw this Foreword to a close, I should perhaps note for the reader's benefit the manner in which students doing course work with me are asked to read the monographs in this series, though I should stress that the books were deliberately designed to be picked up and read in any order one likes. In the first of the two semester courses, called *Language and Learning*, students are asked to read the following volumes in the order given:

Frances Christie − *Language education*
Clare Painter − *Learning the mother tongue*
M.A.K. Halliday & Ruqaiya Hasan − *Language, context, and text: aspects of language in a social-semiotic perspective*
J.L. Lemke − *Using language in the classroom*
then either,
M.A.K. Halliday − *Spoken and written language*
or,
Ruqaiya Hasan − *Linguistics, language, and verbal art.*

The following four volumes, together with the one by Michael Christie, mentioned above, belong to the second course called *Sociocultural Aspects of Language and Education*, and they may be read by the students in any order they like, though only three of the five need be selected for close study:

David Butt − *Talking and thinking: the patterns of behaviour*
Gunther Kress − *Linguistic processes in sociocultural practice*
J.R. Martin − *Factual writing: exploring and challenging social reality*
Cate Poynton − *Language and gender: making the difference*

References

Bain, A., *An English Grammar* (Longman, Roberts and Green, London, 1863).

Bain, A., *English Composition and Rhetoric*, revised in two Parts — *Part 1, Intellectual Elements of Style*, and *Part 11, Emotional Qualities of Style* (Longman, Green and Company, London, 1887).

Ballard, P., *Teaching the Mother Tongue* (Hodder & Stoughton, London, 1921).

Blair, H., *Lectures on Rhetoric and Belles Lettres, Vols. 1 and 11* (W. Strahan and T. Cadell, London, 1783).

Campbell, G., (new ed.), *The Philosophy of Rhetoric* (T. Tegg and Son, London, 1838). Originally published (1776).

Halliday, M.A.K., *Language as social semiotic: the social interpretation of language and meaning* (Edward Arnold, London, 1978).

Halliday, M.A.K., *An Introduction to Functional Grammar* (Edward Arnold, London, 1985).

Murray, Lindley, *English Grammar* (1795), Facsimile Reprint No. 106 (Menston, Scolar Press, 1968).

Contents

Prologue

So what's all the fuss about?

The Plain Speaker: And what are you working on at the moment?

The Linguist: Well, I'm writing a paper on language and gender.

The Plain Speaker: You mean all that stuff about sexist words that feminists carry on about? Now that's something that really irritates me, all this nonsense about *chairperson* and *he* or *she* and *Ms*. If women want to chair meetings that's OK by me, but I don't see why they can't just be called chairmen and shut up about it. And quite frankly the next time someone adds *or she* when I've used *he*, I'll explode!

It's a waste of time, those extra words, and what's more important, it distracts attention from what I'm talking about. When I'm talking, I want to be able to say what I want to say in the quickest and simplest and most straightforward way. I don't want people putting words into my mouth and telling me I shouldn't say this and can't say that—or injecting sex into everything, insisting on a *she* for every *he*!

The Linguist: But if people aren't reminded that *he* could be *she*, it might not occur to them. I remember how taken aback you were when your daughter said she couldn't be a doctor because she was a girl. And how you said she must have picked up such an idea at school because she would never have heard any such nonsense at home.

The Plain Speaker: But what's that got to do with *he* or *she*? That was just some nonsensical idea she picked up from somewhere, which we nipped in the bud before it went any further. We told her in no uncertain terms that it was nonsense. Being a girl wouldn't stop her being a doctor, but not working hard enough at school jolly well would!

The Linguist: I'm afraid I don't share your faith that simply saying something is nonsense means the end of it. And if there's any picking up done between people and ideas, then it's probably more true to say that ideas pick up people rather than the other way round.

The Plain Speaker: What an extraordinary thing to say! That's tantamount to saying that I don't think my own thoughts—my thoughts think me!

The Linguist: Well, I suppose you could put it like that. The trouble is that people think of thoughts or ideas as some kind of invisible things that simply wear words like we wear our clothes. I don't believe that your telling your daughter she can be a doctor if she wants to will make her believe it, because I don't believe that the 'idea' girls-can't-be-doctors means much more than that we live in a society in which people talk about doctors as *he*. Just as nurses are *she*. But it goes further. We see doctoring as male, and nursing as female. We've divided our whole world up into male and female and we then proceed to talk people into making the 'right' choices (or feeling guilty about not having made them) depending on which set of genitals they happen to be born with.

The Plain Speaker [sceptical]: And who's supposed to do the persuading, if we're talked into all this stuff?

The Linguist: We do it ourselves—much of the time without even realising it. Just by learning to talk. It's all in the language.

2

Chapter 1

Language and the social construction of gender

Introduction

Contemporary feminism has focused much attention on the issues of socialisation into gender roles and of sexist discourse. These issues are profoundly interrelated, since the everyday discourse with which children are surrounded from the day of their birth, in which they themselves become eventual participants, is a primary means by which socialisation is effected. Much of the meaning conveyed about what it is to be female and male in late twentieth-century Australian society is conveyed indirectly, implicitly, as we shall see below, but is none the less effective for that. In fact, implicit meanings are undoubtedly more effective, insofar as they remain unquestioned, and hence unproblematic.

Feminists, in particular, have questioned social attitudes and social practice concerning gender and, by doing so, have rendered problematic what was previously, for many, entirely uncontentious—a non-issue. By naming certain attitudes and behaviour **sexist**, a word that did not exist until very recently, attention has been focused on those attitudes and behaviour in a way that was not previously possible.

The feminist stance, speaking on behalf of women, has been highly critical of contemporary society. Feminists have seen women's interests as consistently subordinated to those of men, women's personalities systematically distorted in the service of their subordination, women's capacities underrated or denied, their desire for autonomy frustrated and ridiculed, their sexuality at one and the same time denied, feared, and exploited, and their image trivialised and sentimentalised.

Much of the response to this comprehensive naming of social injustice with respect to women has been to deny that any injustice is involved, to deny that the issue of gender is in any way problematic: men are men, women are women, and that's that. The basis of such denial of the problematic nature of gender is usually that male and female are seen as fundamental, natural, self-evident categories (for some, they have the even greater force of being regarded as God-given categories), whose naturalness and obviousness depends on seeing the social category of gender as deriving automatically and exclusively from the biological category of sex. Thus males are masculine because they have penises and (in the best Freudian tradition) females are feminine because they don't, rather than because they do have clitorises and vaginas.

There is no doubt that the biological difference between male and female is of considerable importance in human societies. It seems equally beyond doubt that what is regarded as appropriate behaviour for males and females, other than that directly consequent on those biological differences (such as insemination, pregnancy, lactation), differs widely from one society to another. It is also readily observable that even where social expectations are strong and explicit, some variability in the behaviour of males and females does occur: many will conform to expected patterns of behaviour, but some (exceptions, deviates, those possessed by devils — the label depending on the society) will not.

All of this suggests that biological **sex** (identification as female or male) needs to be distinguished from social **gender** (identification as feminine or masculine), since the latter is not an automatic consequence of the former.

✗ If gender is a social creation, then one should be able to find evidence that this is so, including evidence of the process of its creation. In particular, one should be able to find linguistic evidence, since language is the primary means by which we create the categories that subsequently come to organise our lives for us. Such evidence is indeed to be found: from the different treatment by parents of newborn babies, depending on sex; through the reiterated messages given to four-year-olds that women and women's activities are marginal and trivial (Hasan, 1986); through the social approval of the writing of little girls at school who write almost exclusively about home and family, elves and fairies, and talking animals while their male classmates get on with the business of finding out how the world outside school and family works and produce what stories they write with the twin focuses of power and violence; through TV, films, and books; to the categories taken for granted in everyday conversation. ʳ

ʸ Difference is simply assumed, with no awareness of the extent to which adult behaviour creates that difference. If it were simply a matter of difference, however, where men and women had their own spheres of activity with rights and status and a complete range of possibilities for achievement within those spheres, then one might feel less concerned. But however much some groups and individuals might like to maintain that this is indeed the case in our society, it is not so.

Three consequences of this differentiation in our society should be of concern:

1. The institutionalised inequality/inferiority of women, where they have been denied the right to engage in certain activities—to be certain kinds of people—and their activitiés and their very selves denigrated and trivialised.
2. The institutionalised channelling of human diversity along two and only two pathways, the choice determined only by which set of genitalia one happens to be born with, with the consequent damage to, and misery of, individuals who, for a variety of reasons, fail to fulfil the stereotyped expectations, to say nothing of the loss to society itself of diverse talents.

See Oakley (1972); Archer & Lloyd (1982).

sex: identification as female or male (biological) gender: identification as feminine or masculine (social)

4

3. The institutionalised hostility between male and female (a complex consequence of both the above). This hostility is most frequently realised in action by male against female, as, for example, in the violation of the right to personal space tellingly portrayed in the following extract from Gerald Murnane's *Tamarisk Row*, an account of a boy's growing up in an Australian provincial town.

> Clement asks—don't you ever try to visit the girls' place to see what they do there? Dillon says—not when the girls are there of course but the other Saturday after the tarts had gone we sneaked down and smashed their place to bits—now if they go down there they can only sit and stare at things or tell girls' secrets to each other or cry all the afternoon because they've lost the place they thought no one knew about.
>
> (Murnane, 1977, p. 87)

A more extreme violation of female by male is the violation of self/identity that is rape. Such hostility is all too commonly discernible, however, in the everyday words of girls and boys, men and women, with respect to one another, words flung in one another's faces or muttered with anger or resentment behind one another's backs.

These issues are of importance to all members of our society, but they should be of particular concern to parents and to educators, because they are the primary agents of the society in the socialisation of children into these institutionalised attitudes. It is at their hands that children learn their initial categorisations of the world they live in, including the evaluations attached to those categorisations. It is from their mouths that children hear the words, and the ways of speaking, that will eventually become their words, their ways of speaking. Children do not remain passive recipients of the socialisation efforts of others but become active agents of their own socialisation as they acquire command of the meanings available to them through command of the words and ways of speaking of those around them.

We need to know what it is we are teaching our children to think and feel about themselves and about each other as female and male, and what are the means by which they have come to learn to think and feel thus. Much of the public debate, such as it is, arising from feminist critiques of language in relation to gender has focused on words and word-forms (such as diminutives) that overtly denigrate, trivialise, or exclude women and which assume or cultivate stereotypes of both women and men. The existence of such words is clearly of importance: the usual explanation is that the existence and use of such words and forms of words unambiguously reveals social attitudes and beliefs. One must go further than words, however, in terms of

1. what one takes into consideration as linguistic, as part of language; and
2. how one regards the relationship between language and thought/ideas/beliefs.

These two issues will be addressed in the next two sections of this chapter.

5

Language and the making of meaning

Much of the discussion of language in relation to sexism has focused on words (LEXIS). Well-known examples include the following: *chairman* and its alternatives, such as *chairperson*; *Ms* as an alternative to *Miss* and *Mrs*; and the use of the pronoun *he* for referring to a person who could be female or male (generic reference) and alternatives such as *he* or *she* and *s/he*. This focus is understandable, since lexis is the most accessible part of language to those not trained as linguists and since it seems that it is lexis that conveys meaning, which is what we're really interested in. Such an approach is inadequate, however: it does not get to grips with the real issues of language in relation to gender, and it makes it very easy for the whole matter to be trivialised (by being seen merely as a matter of alternative labels) or denied (by people saying that they didn't intend any insult or slight in using the words they did, so any offence taken must be in the mind of the hearer).

There are two interrelated problems with approaching language and sexism solely in terms of lexis. The first problem is that this approach ignores other linguistic units and levels, all of which work together to make meaning. The second is that it assumes that language is outside the individual self and even outside the culture in which individuals live, whereas in fact neither would exist without language.

The model that will be used here will be outlined in two stages in this section: firstly a brief account of linguistic units and levels that should be thought of as the basic resources available for the making of meaning, followed by an outline of the set of factors that must be taken into account if we are to understand the actual meanings of the language used by anyone on a particular occasion.

This section is intended as an overview, giving you some insight into the model as a whole, and will be supplemented by introductions to the chapters that follow that will elaborate further on some of the key terms used here.

Linguistic structures

Language as a scientifically describable resource for making meaning can be looked at from three different but interrelated points of view. It can be considered in terms of grammatical structure, where one is interested in how sentences are constructed from smaller units, including words. It can be considered in terms of its physical substance—in the case of speech, this means looking at speech sounds, rhythm, and intonation. It can be considered in relation to the construction of texts (which are not just sets of sentences in any old order): here one is interested in the different ways in which texts of different kinds are linked together as coherent wholes.

Any stretch of language can be described in all three ways: in terms of how it hangs together as a text, in terms of the grammatical structure of the individual sentences within it, and in terms of how it is all realised in terms of speech sounds, rhythm, and intonation. Language can be said to have three levels, or strata, corresponding to these kinds of description: DISCOURSE dealing with the construction of texts; LEXICO-

GRAMMAR dealing with the construction of clauses; PHONOLOGY dealing with getting it all on the air waves. (In the case of written texts, the physical medium is visual rather than aural, so an alternative physical level, GRAPHOLOGY, is needed.)

These strata are represented diagrammatically in Figure 1.1. Each stratum has units particular to it. For example, **clause** (or sentence) and **word** are units of lexico-grammar. The individual units of any stratum will not be introduced here, but where necessary, in the relevant sections below.

Figure 1.1   Language strata

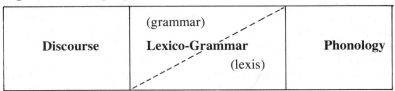

Let us assume then that we have a text — a bit of conversation over the breakfast table or a piece of writing done by a student. And let us assume that we have analysed it exhaustively in terms of its phonology (or graphology), its lexico-grammar, and its discourse features. Such a description of a text would still have limited value if one is interested in the total meaning of that text. We need to go further. Firstly we need to make explicit that constructing texts involves making choices on all the linguistic strata, so that part of the meaning of a text derives from the fact that certain choices were made rather than others that could have been made. For example, part of the meaning of an utterance like *Hang on a tick will you* derives from the fact that it is imperative rather than interrogative and that it uses some colloquial words (*hang on*, *tick*) rather than more neutral or even formal ones. The speaker could have made other choices, producing utterances such as

Wait a minute would you?

or

Would you mind waiting a minute?

The fact that s/he made the particular choices they did, and the kinds of meanings implicated in those choices, needs to be explained. This can best be done by going outside linguistic structure itself and asking questions about what factors influence the actual choices we make in using language, given that we cannot make entirely random choices if we want to be understood by others.

For a discussion of the *s/he* pronoun form, see Chapter 3, p. 49.

Higher level semiotics

There would appear to be three kinds of constraining factors, each of which will be regarded here as a semiotic (meaning-making) system in its own right. These semiotic systems are called REGISTER, GENRE, and IDEOLOGY. These systems do have meanings of their own, but have no means of expression: they have to 'borrow' linguistic forms in order to realise their meanings. Thus the meaning of whatever we say will include register, genre, and ideology meanings. To put it another way, understanding the meaning of what someone says involves much more than knowing what the words refer to: it involves understanding how what is said relates to the context in which it is said (register meanings), what the goal or purpose of the talk is (genre meaning), and what beliefs and values are implicated (ideological meanings). The relationship between language itself and these higher semiotic planes can be represented diagrammatically as in Figure 1.2.

The first semiotic plane above language is **register**. The concern of register is with what Malinowski called **context of situation**: in order to understand a piece of language, one has to know what the institutional context of the discourse is (education, tennis, politics), what the relationship is between speaker and addressee(s), and what channel is being used in order to communicate (the classic example here being the choice between speech and writing). The terms used for these situational, or register, variables are FIELD, TENOR, and MODE respectively, and one of the most powerful aspects of Halliday's linguistic theory, which forms the basis for the model being used here, is the relationship he posits between these register categories and the three major clusters of choices that are involved in the grammatical structure of clauses. Thus field is realised by experiential choices; tenor, by interpersonal choices; and mode, by textual choices. Very recent work on register is making it clear that not only can one predict in this general way what metafunction is associated with which register variable, but much more specifically, one can predict what particular combination of linguistic choices within that metafunction will be implicated. For example, degrees of politeness or deference (tenor choices) will be realised by particular choices of mood, modality, and vocation (terms of address). Contrast the following:

> Answer the phone, stupid
> Can you answer the phone, dear
> Could I get you to answer the phone for me if you wouldn't mind, Mr Tsounis

Although it is now possible to predict more and more precisely what kinds, and what combinations, of linguistic choices will be used to realise register meanings, such predictions will seldom be absolute or categorical. Rather, certain choices, and combinations of choices, will occur with varying probabilities. In other words, we can't predict exactly what will be said in a particular context, but we can say quite a lot about the kinds of linguistic choices involved and the likelihood of their being made.

This means that we can account for a considerable amount of what any instance of language means by examining the structure of the text itself and by looking at the particular choices of field, tenor, and mode as these are realised linguistically. We cannot account for all the meaning of most naturally-occurring texts with just these two levels, however. The next plane, **genre** (an extension of the literary use of this term), has therefore been proposed by J.R. Martin and others working with him at the University of Sydney. If one takes, as Halliday does, the text as the basic unit of meaning, then there is a kind of structuring of texts that has not yet been accounted for and that has to do with the fact that texts mostly don't just start and stop arbitrarily: they go somewhere in terms of having

A detailed discussion of register is given in Halliday & Hasan (1989).

Most of this work is still in progress. The most accessible source will be Martin & Plum.

See Martin (1986)

See Halliday & Hasan (1989).

8

Figure 1.2 Language and its connotative semiotics

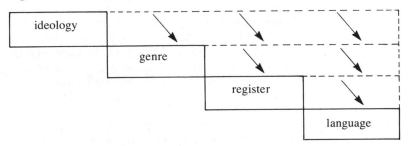

a beginning-middle-end structure and they go somewhere in terms of having a goal, or point. The structures and the goals of genres are specific to particular cultures, i.e. what seems entirely normal, rational, structured behaviour in one culture may seem entirely without point or simply boring to observers from another culture. Hence one can define genres as structured or staged ways of getting things done by means of language in a particular culture. In our society, such staged, goal-oriented activities include making an appointment, writing an essay, conducting a cross-examination in a courtroom, running a committee meeting, interviewing a parent on parent–teacher night, teaching a lesson, recounting key events of the day to someone close to you, writing a story, making a speech, buying a newspaper from the corner shop, telling a joke.

These issues are discussed at length in Halliday & Hasan (1989). See also Martin (1984).

Genres are identifiable by means of the particular linguistic choices that realise their elements of schematic structure (beginning-middle-end structure). Some of these realisations are so characteristic that they uniquely identify the genre: for example, 'Once upon a time . . .' opening the Orientation element of a Narrative. But most of them will be probabilistic; for example, the Complication of a Narrative will consist largely of temporally related material processes, 'They did this and then that and then . . .', up to the point where something goes wrong or something unexpected happens. At this point, material or action process clauses are likely to be displaced by other process types, if the reactions of the protagonists to the crisis are presented by the narrator.

See Rothery (1980, 1984) on the elements of schematic structure of narrative.

Genres are not only realised directly by language; they may also be realised through register. Of all the possible combinations of field, tenor, and mode, any culture recognises only some as constituting appropriate cultural behaviour. Thus the combination music (field), status-marked relationship (tenor), and face-to-face extended monologue as in a lecture (mode) is a possible combination in this culture. No one would think there was anything strange about lecturing on music. If one changes the field to sport, however, many people would start feeling that the lecture was not an appropriate mode choice. Think of those who feel that universities should not have departments of drama, physical education, or domestic science, much less dance or cooking, and yet are perfectly happy to regard foreign languages as an appropriate field for the conduct of lectures and research.

Some of the holes or gaps in the pattern of particular register variable combinations are quite accidental. Frequently such accidental gaps are a function of the availability of appropriate technology. For example, the particular mode choice involving one-way communication,

9

both aural and visual, that has become available as a result of the invention of television is not available in all societies, but there is no barrier other than availability of the technology to this mode option becoming available. In the case of other gaps, there would seem to be considerable barriers to filling them, and much of this opposition would appear to stem from the final semiotic plane to be dealt with: **ideology.**

Despite what is now a formidable array of analytical tools, we do need this last level to account fully for the meaning of most texts. There will be some texts that can be totally accounted for without this last level—but I suspect not many. Consider two examples at very different levels. The first is from a news broadcast concerning the arrest of striking mine workers in Britain where a certain number of individuals were reported as having been arrested 'from a mob of about two thousand'. The choice of the word *mob*, rather than *crowd*, *gathering*, *throng*, *multitude*, etc., implies a particular rather pejorative attitude towards the people concerned. This kind of choice would seem to derive neither from register nor from genre but from some other source of meaning. The second example involves a phenomenon already referred to, the opposition of some people to the inclusion of certain fields as legitimate in tertiary education. Courses dealing with such non-legitimated fields are not uncommonly referred to in derogatory ways, for instance as 'Mickey Mouse courses'. Behind the use of such a label would seem to lie a set of beliefs about the relative importance of fields, just as behind the use of a word like *mob* are a set of beliefs about how people ought to behave in public and what are legitimate reasons for people to gather in public places, together with a set of attitudes towards those who fail to conform to these expectations. Beliefs, attitudes, and values are at the heart of ideology, as the term is being used here.

In particular, most expressions of attitude, or evaluation (judging something as good or bad), are ideological in origin. Such evaluation may be explicit, as when males who act in ways that help to perpetuate the subordinate status of women are referred to as *chauvinists*; or it may take the more implicit form of denying, or attempting to discredit, meanings that threaten the status quo, as when male chauvinists and anti-feminist women persist in responding to feminist claims about sexist language in terms of damage to the language itself (as if language had some value independent of the meanings it enables its speakers to make) or the triviality of the issue—the 'it's only words' response. Evaluation as good or bad, positive or negative, of course depends on ideological position. Thus the feminist who uses *Ms* as a title for all women is making a positive ideological choice, while the male chauvinist sees it as a negative one: anti-man rather than pro-woman.

See the section 'Male vs. female: the ideology of gender' in Chapter 1, pp. 17–20. The section 'Male versus female: the ideology of gender' below will focus specifically on gender as an ideological issue. For the moment I will simply say that ideology deals in evaluation, probably always in relation to binary oppositions such as female/male, capitalism/socialism, war/peace; that in its dynamic aspect it involves favoured genre, register, and language choices in relation to particular issues; that it is not merely a matter of a coherent system of ideas, or 'false consciousness', or any other political or sociological account of ideology, though such notions will need ultimately to be incorporated into a comprehensive account.

10

It is probably true to say that no culture, and no individual within a culture, functions without ideology. However, insofar as we fail to recognise its presence and the oppression and destruction that can be caused because of it, we are failing to take the making of meaning into our own hands. As we shall see in the next section, we construct the reality we inhabit.

Language and the construction of reality

There is an English expression that can be used under rather different circumstances with, apparently, rather different meanings. In a foreign country, a meeting with a compatriot with whom one may, under other circumstances, have little in common can be a great pleasure precisely because it is a meeting between people who 'speak the same language'. In one's own country, among familiar surroundings (social, geographical, and linguistic), one may also use precisely the same expression to indicate a special closeness or bond between people by saying that they 'speak the same language'.

At first glance, it looks as if the first use of this expression is literal while the second is metaphorical. In fact, both are to be taken literally, though in slightly different ways. In the first instance, the more physical aspects of speech (its characteristic sounds, rhythms, and intonation) are a very evident element of the satisfaction of such encounters, but a less conscious awareness of, and response to, such features is undoubtedly present in interaction between those who feel themselves particularly close within their own society. The difference is one of degree: when one is overseas, sounding Australian (even stereotypically so) is what triggers recognition, whereas at home it will probably be sounding like a certain kind of Australian—my kind, someone I can feel comfortable with.

Beyond this physical level (the level of expression), however, are various content dimensions that are commonly regarded not as matters of language at all, but as manifestations of **personality** (either individual or national). In explaining what we mean when we say we 'speak the same language', we may refer to 'having a similar sense of humour', 'knowing when to say something and when to just shut up', 'being interested in the same things', 'thinking the same way about things', 'having the same values/attitudes', 'knowing what the other is going to say before they've said it', 'being on the same wavelength', 'always saying the right thing', or 'not always having to explain yourself'.

Such expressions taken individually seem to refer to skills and/or knowledge possessed by individual speakers. When one puts together such expressions, however, one seems to be talking of something much larger than a particular skill, and something that is shared between speakers: a whole world-view, a set of beliefs about the way things are and ought to be (in particular about things knowable and things sayable), a body of knowledge about not simply what matters and what doesn't, but about what is real and what isn't.

Language plays a crucial role in the construction of the shared view of reality held by speakers of a common language in three interrelated ways:

1. by naming aspects of the physical and social reality speakers inhabit that are seen as significant in a particular culture;
2. through the ways of speaking that are characteristic of a particular culture, not only insofar as named aspects of the culture are embedded within them but particularly insofar as they make possible the enactment of social institutions and social values;
3. through covert grammatical categories (Whorf, 1956), particularly when these form congruent sets, which Martin (1988) calls grammatical 'conspiracies'.

Naming reality

Naming is essentially a matter of lexis (words). The presence or absence of certain words is most frequently cited as evidence of similarity or difference between cultures, and sub-cultures, but it is not entirely clear how important lexis is in the construction of reality. Martin's view is that lexis is so flexible, in that it can be added to at any time if changed circumstances warrant, that 'if anything **determines** speakers' particular world views, it is not the conscious, specific part of their language—its lexical structure' (Martin, 1988, p. 2).

In many areas of the lexicon this is undoubtedly true, but in ideologically sensitive areas one may find gaps, or even misnaming, together with strong resistance to any attempts at filling the gaps or correcting the misnaming. One kind of gap, involving the literal existence of a name or names that may be known to only a few or that must never be used, is due to taboo, for example, children being given names for all their body parts except the genitals, which are simply referred to as *down there*. The phenomenon more properly called a gap, or hole, involves the total absence of any kind of lexical item referring to a particular aspect of experience. Some gaps seem to be quite accidental and arbitrary and remain unfilled even when social difficulties are created by the lack of a word or words (for example, in English, the absence of specific terms of address for one's parents-in-law creates no end of social awkwardness). Some gaps only open up under changed circumstances (due to migration or new technology, for instance) and these are generally speedily filled. Others again only begin to be seen as gaps when resistance to the pressure of a powerful ideology begins to bring about a questioning of the status quo. Thus, aspects of social reality that come to be perceived as oppressive by those who are oppressed may come to be named by them. For example, women moved on from Betty Friedan's initial 'problem that has no name' (Friedan, 1965, title of opening chapter), to 'naming' that problem as *patriarchy* (new meaning for old word) or *sexism* (an entirely new word). Likewise those who come to perceive oppression, and no longer wish to act as agents of it, may 'name' what they see as going on. For example, some teachers and educationalists began to name the *hidden curriculum* of schooling.

The difficulty is that if one has grown up surrounded by a particular set of 'messages' or 'instructions' about how one should see, think, feel, act, and talk about the nature and purposes of the social institutions in which one is involved, it is extremely difficult to even conceive of the possibility of there being a vantage point from which one might see things differently, much less to actually situate oneself at such a strategic place. The most recent wave of feminist social commentators have had much to say on how so many aspects of women's experience have been misnamed or not named at all, putting women who did not experience their lives as they were supposed to in the intolerable position of taking personal responsibility for their inadequacy in being unable to live out the ideological requirements of the culture. The nineteenth- and twentieth-century cult of the child is another instance of ideological naming that distorts the experience of children and adult perceptions of children and their experience (Ariès, 1973; Steedman, 1982).

Kress and Hodge note that naming does not only lead to familiarity with, and easier classification and memory of, what is named but that 'only what has a name can be shared'. They go on to say:

> Language fixes a world that is so much more stable and coherent than what we actually see that it takes its place in our consciousness and becomes what we think we have seen. And since normal perception works by constant feedback, the gap between the real world and the socially constructed world is constantly being reduced, so that what we do 'see' tends to become what we can say.
>
> (Kress & Hodge, 1979, p.5)

Or, indeed, what we habitually do say becomes what we 'see'. Consider a piece of research conducted by John and Sandra Condry that set out to investigate whether the behaviour of a nine-month-old infant would be labelled differently, depending on whether observers thought they were observing a girl or a boy. The child was shown on video responding to four stimuli (a teddy-bear, a doll, a jack-in-the-box, and a buzzer) and subjects were asked to rate the child's behaviour in terms of three emotional dimensions (pleasure, anger, and fear).

Overall, when the infant was thought to be a boy, it 'was seen as displaying more pleasure and less fear' than when it was thought to be a girl (Condry & Condry, 1976, p. 817). The more disturbing finding, however, concerned reactions to the child's response to the jack-in-the-box, which Condry and Condry regarded as a more 'ambiguous' situation than the others, that is, as less obviously likely to give rise to positive or negative responses. They commented:

> We found that the 'negative' emotion displayed was labeled 'anger' if the infant was thought to be a boy, and 'fear' if the infant was thought to be a girl . . . The direction of the effect suggests what might happen next, to wit: If you think a child is **angry** do you treat 'him' differently than if you think 'she' is **afraid**? . . . It seems reasonable to assume that a child who is thought to be afraid is held and cuddled more than a child who is thought to be angry. Regardless of the direction of the difference, if future research shows treatment differences, these could highlight an important causal sequence in the development of sex differences.
>
> (Condry & Condry, 1976, pp. 817, 818)

What the subjects in this study 'saw' can only be explained in terms of a classification of female and male that habitually associates certain attributes with one gender but not the other. Such habitual associations are coded linguistically in structures consisting of adjective and noun (stereotypic examples would be *pretty girl*, *brave boy*) or, even more covertly, in nouns that one doesn't even recognise as being part of such a covert grammatical category of gender until one has to choose an appropriate pronoun to stand for such a noun. (The question of covert gender will be dealt with further below, under the heading 'Covert grammatical categories'.)

See also the section 'Grammatical structure: the nominal group' in Chapter 4, pp. 57–62.

Ways of speaking

Naming, in its various guises, is embedded most unproblematically in everyday informal conversation, where it is what gets taken for granted that is significant for the construction of reality. Berger and Luckman consider conversation to be 'the most important vehicle of reality-maintenance' and go on to elaborate this statement as follows:

> One may view the individual's everyday life in terms of the working away of a conversational apparatus that ongoingly maintains, modifies and reconstructs his subjective reality . . . The greater part of reality-maintenance in conversation is implicit, not explicit. Most conversation does not in so many words define the nature of the world. Rather, it takes place against the background of a world that is silently taken for granted. Thus an exchange such as, 'Well, it's time for me to get to the station', and 'Fine, darling, have a good day at the office', implies an entire world **within which** these apparently simple propositions make sense. By virtue of this implication the exchange confirms the subjective reality of this world.
>
> If this is understood, one will readily see that the great part, if not all, of everyday conversation maintains subjective reality. Indeed, its massivity is achieved by the accumulation and consistency of casual conversation— conversation that can **afford to be casual** precisely because it refers to the routines of a taken-for-granted world.
>
> (Berger & Luckmann, 1966, p. 172)

Berger and Luckmann understand what it is that conversation achieves, but as sociologists rather than linguists, they do not offer any detailed account of how it is done. Systemic linguistics does, however, offer ways in to explaining the how. Halliday sees 'ordinary spontaneous conversations' in very much the way Berger and Luckmann do, speaking of

> the magical power that it has, the power of constructing and organizing social situations, of providing a foundation for interpersonal relations and the socialization process, of maintaining and giving a history to personal identity, and of creating and modifying the structure of reality.
>
> (Halliday, 1984, p.10)

What Halliday does here, and elsewhere, is to demonstrate how the actual linguistic choices (at the levels of discourse, lexico-grammar, and phonology) are realisations of acts of meaning that are to be understood as 'in the final analysis, the "realization" of choices at some higher level, somewhere in the semiotic systems of the culture' (Halliday, 1984, p.10). Members of the Register Working Group at the University of Sydney are currently working on formalising the systems of choices of

See entries for Martin, Plum, Poynton, Rothery, Thwaite, and Ventola in the References.

such higher level semiotics, identified as register, genre, and ideology (introduced in the preceding section), and their work has been drawn on heavily in putting together this account of language and gender. (See references for Martin, Plum, Poynton, Rothery, Thwaite and Ventola.)

'Ordinary spontaneous conversation' is not the only way of speaking, however. As has been indicated in the preceding section, and as will be dealt with at greater length in Chapter 2, there is a range of ways of speaking, or genres, that are available within a particular society. Some of these may occur embedded within conversation, for example, Recount (relating a series of events), Exposition (arguing a case for a point of view), and Narrative (a temporally organised series of events that involves a crisis or complication that has to be resolved). Other genres occur quite independently of ordinary conversation (or may have conversation embedded in them, for example, service encounters) and some of them are learned as part of the process of taking on particular social roles (such as that of shop-steward, teacher, barrister, or post-office clerk). All genres are learned as ways of enacting social processes that are functional in the society in which they take place. Insofar as any individual will only learn some genres, will have some familiarity with others, and may not even know of the existence of yet more outside those parts of the society s/he functions in, and has access to, then genre too plays an important role in the relationship between the individual, language, and society.

The work of Basil Bernstein (1971, 1973, 1975) should be mentioned here because he is vitally concerned with the question of differential access to meaning dependent on class (one particular kind of sub-culture within a society) and with the educational consequences of this. His pioneering insights into the importance of socialisation through talk within particular sub-cultures met with considerable criticism and much damaging misrepresentation at the time his work first became widely known, but they are now being vindicated as more appropriate kinds of linguistic analysis than Bernstein had to work with become available. Indeed some of the linguistic tools now available have been developed because of the nature of the work he was interested in, and because of the need to find appropriate support for it.

Covert grammatical categories

We now move from language as social process back into the heart of the linguistic system itself and the question of whether there is anything in 'the structure of a language that predisposes certain ways of seeing the world or certain ways of acting in it' (Martin, 1988, p.1). The American linguist B.L. Whorf, through his identification of what he called **cryptotypes** (hidden or covert grammatical features), which he related to aspects of the culture, demonstrated that linguistic structure could indeed contribute to one's world-view. As Martin points out, Whorf put most weight in making his case on those issues where sets of categories 'which cumulatively oriented speakers in a certain direction' were involved (Martin, 1988, p.3). It is such sets of categories that Martin calls grammatical 'conspiracies'. Whorf worked with American Indian languages, Martin's paper deals with Tagalog, and both have demonstrated that such grammatical conspiracies can indeed be found. Whorf's best known work deals with how **time** is handled in Hopi society, the Hopi language grammaticalising time very differently from European languages, and Martin brings together a range of morphological, grammatical, and discourse phenomena that seem to be intimately related to three important themes or elements of Philippine society, which he calls **family**, **face**, and **fate**.

When one turns to English, there is certainly evidence of a grammatical conspiracy as far as **gender** is concerned. Kress and Hodge (1979, pp. 77-82) detail some of this evidence. They point out that English does not, like many languages, have an overt category of gender (requiring that all nouns, and, in some languages, adjectives and other parts of speech, be identified as masculine, feminine, or neuter) but that it does have a covert category revealed in ways such as:

1. pronoun choice with reference to certain common nouns (e.g. countries, ships, and some cars are *she*). See Whorf (1956), who first identified the covert category in English by this pronoun test, and MacKay and Konishi (1980), who examined personification in children's literature and found that 'antecedents of *he* tended to be strong, active, brave, wise, clever, and mischievous, while antecedents of *she* tended to be weak, passive, and foolish' (p. 149);
2. adjective choice with reference to males or females, or products associated with them. Kress and Hodge examine adjectives used in advertising that have what they call feminine or masculine **valency**. They propose the following 'abstract schema for femininity', in which they see the defining categories as constituting the ideology.

Table 1.1 Schema for femininity

Defining categories	Typical qualities	Feminine nouns	Feminine verbs
− active + weak + obedient + pleasing + caring	Adjectives implying one or more defining categories	Nouns with preferred linkages with feminine adjectives	Verbs with preferred feminine agents

Source: Kress & Hodge (1979), p.81

Further evidence for the existence of at least a covert category, if not a conspiracy, regarding gender in English comes from my work on personal names and on familiar or diminutive forms of words, including names (Poynton, 1984b). Personal names would seem to constitute a class with overt gender, with only a few instances of names that can be either female or male (and many of these make the gender clear when written down). The two gender classes are distinguished with such massive redundancy, however, (including phonological differences, different relationships with other parts of the lexicon, different potentials for borrowing from other languages, different degrees of freedom for orthographic variation) that it really does seem like a case of protesting too much: gender does not need to be marked over and over again.

Grammatical conspiracies are undoubtedly the least accessible way in which language affects our view of reality, but they are of the utmost importance if we are to understand that 'society, language and mind are indissoluble: society creates mind, mind creates society, and language stands as mediator and metaphor for both these processes' (Halliday, 1977, p. 31).

Male versus female: the ideology of gender

The nature and genesis of ideology

Returning now to the notion of ideology, left rather undeveloped at the end of the section 'Higher level semiotics' above, the first thing that needs to be considered is whether **ideology** is simply another way of referring to the **world-view** of a particular culture. The term 'ideology' certainly seems to be used in this way, meaning the body of ideas characteristic of a particular society or sub-culture. This seems to be the approach of Kress and Hodge when they observe that:

See pp. 7–11.

> Language, typically, is immersed in the ongoing life of a society, as the practical consciousness of that society. This consciousness is inevitably a partial and false consciousness. We can call it ideology, defining 'ideology' as a systematic body of ideas, organized from a particular point of view. Ideology is thus a subsuming category which includes sciences and metaphysics, as well as political ideologies of various kinds, without implying anything about their status and reliability as guides to reality.
>
> (Kress & Hodge, 1979, p.6)

Smith (1973) prefers to use the term **cosmology**, which he defines as 'the set of beliefs concerning how things are' (Smith 1973, p.106). He is quite explicit, however, that this is identical with **world-view**, the term usually associated with language. Smith's notion of an ideological system incorporates not merely 'knowledge', however, but also value and attitude systems. He sees the ideological system as consisting of:

> The set of rules which an individual has acquired for making judgments about things or behaviours he experiences. Therefore it is the culture system that engenders what can be termed esthetic or ethical modes of behavior.
>
> . (Smith, 1973, p.105)

The addition of this evaluative dimension to the notion of ideology as cosmology, or world-view, is important, as we shall see.

Smith, unlike Kress and Hodge, however, fails to address the question of the origins of ideology. The classic interpretation of ideology, derived from Marx, is that it is 'systematic distortion in the service of class interest' (Kress & Hodge, 1979, p.6), that distortion functioning to legitimate power relations based on class. Power relations in a society are not exclusively based on class, however. Weber saw status groups and parties, as well as classes, as involving power relations in a society. And feminist theorists such as Juliet Mitchell, as Wearing (1984, p.16) notes, 'have attempted to develop fresh insights into the concept of ideology' by including gender 'as a basis for the generation of ideology'.

The identification of such apparently biologically based categories as gender, and presumably also race, as sources of ideology is a particularly important development in our understanding of the social construction of reality. Having understood that the 'naturalness' and 'inevitability' of power relations based on class is a construct of ideology as a legitimating mechanism, it has become possible to focus attention on other arenas of social life where inequality and downright oppression have been legitimated in terms of the 'naturalness', 'obviousness', and 'inevitability' of 'biological' difference.

The form of ideology

Up to this point, ideology has been referred to as if it were a **thing** of some kind. It makes more sense, however, to speak of the **process** of ideologising, the process of the creation of meanings within a society characterised by certain patterns of control (of other people, of objects—including the means of production, and hence of ideas or knowledge). Hence, ideological meanings emerge out of particular power-configurations. But rather than being separable from the society that has produced them, they mirror that society back to itself in such a way as to reinforce its own identity. In other words, they constitute both the reality and the theory of reality of a society. It is only when the power-configuration is challenged from within or begins to change (due to challenge or external causes) that emphasis comes to be placed on ideology as theory rather than as constitutive of reality. At such times, ideology becomes visible as ideology, rather than being invisible, as the everyday and unchallenged pattern of meanings of a particular society.

What becomes visible will be a pattern derivable from a myriad instances of meanings being made to fit a particular kind of social organisation, a pattern involving, firstly, some kind of **opposition**, or **dichotomy**, and, secondly, an **evaluation** of the terms of that dichotomy such that one term is more highly valued than the other.

The ideological dichotomy at issue here is that of *woman* opposed to *man*. Essentially the same dichotomy, but in somewhat more ideologically transparent form, is found in the opposition of *male* to *female* and even more so in that of *feminine* to *masculine*. This opposition may indeed be 'the primordial opposition on which all others are based' (Culler, 1983, p.165). It is certainly the case that, in its various ideological guises, it invokes an enormous number of dichotomies fundamental not only to this culture but to others (such as the opposition between *yin* and *yang* in Chinese culture). Table 1.2 shows some of the associated oppositions for speakers of English.

Table 1.2 Some oppositions associated with gender in English

Man/Male/Masculine	Woman/Female/Feminine
reason	emotion
active	passive
instrumental	expressive
knowledge	ignorance
competence	incompetence
action	speech
culture	nature

On this last opposition, see MacCormack and Strathern (1980).

18

Some of these oppositions involve a cluster of associated meanings. Thus the reason/emotion opposition incorporates notions of man as rational, logical, reasonable, and in control of his feelings, compared with woman who is irrational, illogical, unreasonable, and emotional (commonly interpreted as excessively so. Less pejoratively, woman is tender-hearted, where man can be callous and unfeeling). And intuition belongs here too, though somewhat ambivalently, depending on whether it is seen as a kind of knowledge (albeit arrived at without conscious effort on the part of the knower) or as a matter of feeling—'I just felt in my bones . . .'.

The evaluation of these ideological dichotomies, whether single oppositions or clusters, proceeds in two stages. There is an absolute evaluation, which on the whole values more highly the terms associated with the male (especially *reason*, *knowledge*, *action*, and *culture*) by seeing these as fundamental to Western culture, as the values that have enabled it to achieve the kind of control of both the natural and the social worlds that characterises late twentieth-century Western capitalism. The second layer of evaluation is a conditional one, valuing the terms associated with the female (especially *emotion*, *expressiveness*, and *nature*) only insofar as these are not set up as counter-values challenging the ascendancy of the dominant values. In cultural terms, this means that the arts and the natural world may flourish but within definite limits: they must expect neither unlimited funds nor to retain their autonomy (even their existence) if this does not suit those who wield real power.

In personal terms, conditional evaluation means that a subordinate group is only evaluated positively insofar as it lives out its subordination in the ideological terms that have been set up for it. Thus *the good woman* is the wife and mother who supports and nurtures others, feels with and for them, and demands nothing for herself. Similarly, *the good child* is child-like, docile, and innocent, needing the mother's protection. Both *woman* and *child* are ideologically 'not man' in separate but interrelated ways: the infantilisation of the child is a means of both securing a longer period of socialisation of the child, so that s/he may acquire skills and internalise values of advantage to the dominant ideology, and at the same time of enforcing the ideological expectations of women's behaviour.

It is important to understand that women are devalued in the giving of this kind of conditional valuation. Right-wing women who want to value women precisely insofar as they are privatised and domesticated are either ideologically naive, mistaking rhetoric for substance, or else they are prepared to pay the price of restricted life-choices and consequent restricted access to real power in the society in order to retain their sheltered workshops in the home. As long as women who are articulate, intelligent, and eager to achieve in spheres outside the domestic are regarded as aberrant, and in some way suspect in their very status as women, then sexism—the ideology of gender as the 'inferiorization (attitudinal and actual)' (Mitchell, 1971, p. 64) of women with respect to men—is alive and well and likely to continue to play a significant role in the formation of both female and male psyches.

See Ehrenreich (1983), especially Chapter 10, pp. 144–68.

It is not enough, however, to identify an ideological pattern of inferiorisation of women. Many will object that much of this pattern as it has so far been spelt out consists of stereotyped beliefs and attitudes that are not shared by the enlightened and that the actual behaviour of men and women (and the responses accorded that behaviour) has always been more variable than the stereotypes allow for, to say nothing of the fact that considerable changes have taken place (for the better, for women) over the last century. This is all true and yet in a very profound way, it is all beside the point.

Ideological structures are not imposed on the day-to-day reality of ordinary living from the outside, so that individuals can 'choose' whether or not to adopt an ideological position. Ideological structures are merely formalisations of patterns of behaviour characteristic of a particular society. As long as individuals participate in the institutions of that society, they must perforce act ideologically. Hence as long as the four key structures of women's situation—production, reproduction, sexuality, and the socialisation of children (Mitchell, 1971)—remain substantially unchanged, the ideological meanings of *man* and *woman* will remain unchanged.

Those meanings arise in the first instance from the activities of men and women, including, most importantly, their talk about themselves and each other, and the activities of both. The ideological pattern identified above is a way of looking at the significance of the myriad day-to-day activities that men and women engage in and that define them as men and women in the terms of a particular culture: it is an abstraction from the on-going processes of everyday life that enables us to focus on recurrent themes in those processes. We are able to abstract in this way because, firstly, human culture is fundamentally patterned—not random—and, secondly, human language facilitates not merely action but also reflection—it can be turned back on itself, enabling us to use it as a tool to ask questions about the meanings we have already made with it.

Relevant contemporary feminist writing includes Ellmann (1979); Firestone (1972); Greer (1971); Janssen-Jurreit (1982); Millett (1971); Mitchell (1971).

See Einstein (1984) for a useful introduction, especially to American feminist thought.

To really understand the nature and role of a particular ideology in a particular society, then, one needs to adopt two perspectives: a bird's-eye view of the overall pattern, and an understanding of the interactive patterns of everyday life. This section has sketched in some key elements of the overall pattern of meanings made in this society with respect to women and men—the bird's-eye view. This is the perspective that can be found elaborated in considerable detail in contemporary feminist writing. The interactive perspective, concerning the ongoing making of meanings in the course of everyday activities and interactions, will be the focus of the next five chapters, as we investigate the way the ideology of gender is perpetuated by being created anew for each generation by means of what we may (and do) say, how we say it, and what we say it for.

Chapter 2

Using language to achieve social goals

Introduction

In focusing on genre in this chapter, we will be investigating the question of 'how things get done, when language is used to accomplish them', or 'the verbal strategies used to accomplish social purposes of many kinds' (Martin, 1985b, pp. 250, 251).

Genre needs to be examined first because it deals with the question of goals, with what are recognised and socially sanctioned as possible ends or purposes within a particular society. In being socialised into particular cultural identities, involving nationality, ethnicity, class, and gender, individuals learn the set of genres that are available to them and appropriate for them in terms of that national/ethnic/class/gender identity. And in learning the genres, they learn what are possible goals for them. If this learning is successful, then what can happen is that other genres are seen as pointless and meaningless, if their goals contradict in some way the goals already internalised or if one comes upon them with little or no prior orientation to them.

If one learns to mean with only some kinds of goal in mind, then those will become the only possible, real goals. And even if one somehow manages to see other kinds of goal as meaningful and to want to master the appropriate genre, one may find all sorts of barriers placed in one's way. In the case of gender, the blocking of access has often been quite blatant. Think of the struggle of nineteenth-century women to have their novels published—most managed it only by using male pseudonyms, including some of the greatest writers of their time, such as 'George Eliot' (Marian Evans), 'Henry Handel Richardson' (Florence Ethel Richardson), and the Brontë sisters. Or think of the battles women had to gain admission to the bar, or the right to make public speeches, or to be newsreaders on radio or TV.

In our society (as in most), access to and participation in prestigious genres, and consequently evaluation of genres themselves and of genre performance, has historically been determined largely by class and by gender. Thus middle-class and upper-class males predominate in the prestigious genres of the courtroom cross-examination, the Prime Ministerial address to the nation, the university lecture, the political com-

See Heath's (1983) account of the difficulties faced by children from two American Southern working-class communities whose genre competence was not what the schools they attended assumed they had and who consequently were severely educationally disadvantaged.

mentary, the novel (the serious novel, that is, not the thriller, the sci-fi work, or the romance, all of which have lower prestige, and in which, hardly coincidently, many women are acknowledged as excelling). Where women are recognised as having competence in a genre, that genre will tend to have lower prestige or to be distinguished in some way that enables it to be taken less seriously or even pejoratively. Compare the prestige of the *romance* with that of the *serious novel*, or even that of the *pornographic novel*; consider *conversation* in relation to *chat* or *gossip*; ponder the cultural implications of *critique* and *pep-talk* contrasted with *nagging* or *scolding*.

Even more seriously, some genres in which women do have competence are not even recognised as such—they are in effect invisible. Linguists have had to devise terms such as *service-encounter*, *mother/child interaction*, and *classroom interaction* in their descriptions of goal-oriented social processes realised primarily by women—millions of women, every day—because there were no names for these genres in the English language. And where there are no names, no words, for a phenomenon, it can hardly be said to exist: what is not said is not real.

The absence of names for some of the 'staged, goal-oriented, purposeful activities in which speakers engage as members of our culture' (Martin, 1984, p. 25) does need to be qualified slightly. We do have ways of referring to such activities as making an appointment, doing the shopping, teaching, etc. as on-going activities, by the use of appropriate verbs. What we lack are ways of referring to what is produced linguistically in such situations as texts, in the way in which we can refer to the products of other kinds of activity by speakers (or writers) such as *interview*, *sermon*, *essay*, *business letter*, etc. This focus on process rather than product, common with spoken genres, de-emphasises the role played by language in such activities, making it harder to see that they are fundamentally linguistic, even when pared down to this kind of minimal exchange with the bus driver:

Passenger:	Ninety thanks.
Bus Driver:	[Gives ticket and change]
Passenger:	Ta.

No complete taxonomy of genres exists, for any society, but Table 2.1 sets out a range of some of those used by English-speakers, cross classified according to whether they are high or low prestige, and whether they are spoken or written.

Many other dimensions would need to be taken into account in a complete taxonomy, specifically those related to the register categories of field, tenor, and mode. As Martin (1985b) has noted, not all combinations of the values of these register variables are found in a culture at any point in time and such gaps or disjunctions are immensely revealing of the culture. This is particularly so in relation to gender. To take just one example, until very recently, public discourse about female sexuality (field choice) was conducted largely by male scientific experts (tenor choices of unequal power, low (or no) contact, and no (or negative) affect) using written forms (mode choices of language as reflection rather than language as action and monologue, eye contact only, rather than dialogue). Now the range of register options and the number of genres regarded as culturally acceptable are much less constrained as women, in particular, have filled in some of the gaps by talking (as well as writing), about personal experience (as well as physiology), including how they feel about themselves, their bodies, and their sexual partners.

Table 2.1 A selection of genres used by speakers of English

	Low-prestige genres	High-prestige genres
Speech	conversation (chat, gossip)	cross-examination
	sports commentary	interview
	appointment making	sermon
	service encounter	speech (oration)
	(goods, services, information)	lecture
	joke	debate
	riddle	advertisement
	invitation	news broadcast
	recount (= temporally organised	poem
	account of actual events)	submission
	personal letter	report (company, scientific)
	(news, condolence, thank you . . .)	business letter
	recipe	novel
	instruction manual	essay
Writing		treatise

An adequate characterisation of all the genres listed in Table 2.1, to say nothing of the many others not mentioned there, would involve specifying their internal organisation as staged activities having a schematic structure. So far, very few such descriptions are available. Genres that have been so characterised include:

- casual conversation (Ventola, 1979);
- service encounters (inc. post-office, small shop, travel agency) (Hasan, 1979; Ventola, 1983, 1987);
- the range of genres handled by children in their writing (Rothery, in preparation; Martin & Rothery, 1980, 1981);
- medical appointment making (Hasan, 1978);
- some genres of schooling (Christie, 1985a, 1985b, 1985c).

See Halliday & Hasan (1989), Part B.

Partly because of this lack of appropriate descriptions of schematic structure, but largely because the issues of access/participation and evaluation are most relevant to considering genre in relation to gender, the internal organisation of genres will receive little attention in what follows. It needs to be emphasised, however, that genres are ultimately distinguishable on this basis and not on the basis of the presence or absence of apparently genre-referring words in everyday language. Thus the word *story*, used in the infants' or primary-school classroom, can refer to any one of a range of genres without this ever being made explicit (by teachers to themselves, much less to the children they teach), while the set of words *chat*, *gossip*, *natter*, etc. do not refer to distinct genres at all but rather are pejorative ways of referring to a genre that is most neutrally labelled *conversation*, indicating that when conversation is carried on by certain people and/or deals with certain topics, it is regarded as trivial and not worth taking seriously.

The approach adopted here has been to take a number of instances of genres in which children are participants, or have many opportunities for first-hand observation, as the jumping-off point for investigating the interrelationship of genre and gender. Children learn in their earliest years about what language is for from the range of genres they know or know about. That range is taken with them into school and it plays a significant role in determining what they can make sense of, and hence make use of, from the school's repertoire of assumptions about what language is for, the range of genres it expects students to master. And the extent of that mastery in turn has far-reaching consequences for the individuals concerned, girls and boys, men and women, and for the society as a whole.

The world of home and informal interaction

The child is born into a world of words, but it is not the same world for girls and boys, even when newborn. There is the first text occasioned by their arrival:

It's a   (beautiful)   boy!
It's a   (dear little)   girl!

the prelude to the many occasions, particularly in interaction with the mother, when they will be told (or asked rhetorically):

You're a gorgeous girl!
Who's a beautiful boy?

and exhorted to be, or praised for being, good:

Be a good boy.
That's a good girl.

All of this happens, of course, long before children have any comprehension of language or any awareness of themselves as female or male. Their identification as male or female is of crucial cultural importance to those around them, however, and manifests itself immediately in different communicative behaviours with respect to newborn infants. One study indicated that newborn baby girls are given more overt physical attention (looking at, smiling at, touching) than newborn baby boys (Thoman et al., 1972). Other studies have found the following: that there is more vocal-verbal communication between mothers and daughters than between mothers and sons at three months of age (Lewis & Freedle, 1973); that girls in the first two years are more often looked at and talked to than are boys (Lewis, 1972); that mothers playing with two-year-olds are more likely to develop conversations with girls than they are with boys (Cherry, 1975a); that in families with several children, girls are addressed more gently and boys more robustly, especially by fathers (Gleason, 1973); that outside play may be encouraged more for boys than girls, thus decreasing exposure to adult speech, and sex-typed toys may provide more opportunity for girls to model the communicative behaviour of mothers, e.g. in play with dolls, while boys lack adult communicative models in their action-play with trucks, cars, and construction games and use sound effects rather than talk more often than do girls (McCarthy, 1953; Gleason, 1973).

Such findings strongly suggest that girls are sensitised to, and social-ised into, the interactive genre of conversation at a very early age while boys are likely to be less developed in this respect. Since much of the current research on child language development is emphasising the importance of communicative interaction with the child, it is likely that more light will be shed on generic development than has been shed by older child language studies focusing purely on type and number of sounds, words, and structures.

Conversation is crucial to culture in a number of ways, so the con-sequences of differences in socialisation—as far as orientation towards conversation and competence in it are concerned—are enormous. Everyday conversation, as we saw in the section 'Language and the con-struction of reality' above, is crucial in the construction and maintenance See pp. 11–17. of social reality in terms of what is made explicit but also in terms of what is simply taken for granted. Both these kinds of saying, the explicit and the implicit, need to be mastered if the genre itself is to be mastered, and the construction of the self as part of the social reality that is in a constant state of reconstruction is an inevitable consequence of such learning.

Much attention has been focused on explicit messages exhorting children to conform to sex-role expectations (of the 'Boys don't cry/wear dresses', 'Girls shouldn't swear/play with trains' variety). This attention is fully justified, since such messages explicitly code sexist ideology and are learned as part of the meaning of being female or male that children apply first to themselves and then to other children, thereby becoming agents of their own and other children's socialisation into that ideology. There is no reason to assume that children of either gender are more (or less) subject to such coercive messages, which may occur as isolated utterances or as part of ongoing conversation, though the sanctions (dis-approval, punishment) are probably more severe for boys who trans-gress than for girls.

There are two other kinds of message, one somewhat less explicit, but still coded lexically as part of the content of conversation, and the other quite implicit, involving responses to both the form and content of conversation, which may never be lexicalised at all, where girls would seem to be more at risk. Both types of message are clearly implicated in gender-role formation, but the focus is not on what is expected of the child as male or female but rather on how adults, female and male, see themselves and the activities they habitually engage in.

Hasan, in a study of mother–child talk (Hasan, 1986), found that mothers consistently underplayed the positive aspects of their multiple mothering role of instructor/labourer/emotional support and companion. In 25 real hours of speech, there was no instance of a mother claiming credit for solving a problem—in fact many of them presented themselves as 'silly Mummy', thereby perpetuating the stereotype of women as lacking in intellect. Fathers could be 'clever Daddy' but there was no 'clever Mummy'. Women's attitudes to their work within the home were even more revealing. Women's work was presented explicitly as uninteresting, but only obliquely as hard (nearly three-quarters of the women mentioned tiredness at some time or another). Children in their everyday lives must experience their mothers' busyness. But if this

25

experience is not first linguistically confirmed and then positively evaluated by mothers, it is extremely unlikely, in the short term at least, that children will come to see what mothers do as work, or even as important.

Mothers who pass on such 'knowledge' of female inferiority to their children have themselves internalised it from just such messages as they are now passing on to their children, from explicit messages concerning male superiority and, most subtly of all, from male responses to female conversation.

One of the persistent stereotypes of women as language users is that they are indefatigable talkers. A host of lexical items testifies to this belief and to the negative evaluation of women as talkers: they are *gossips*, *chatterers*, *prattlers*, *gas-bags*, *chatterboxes* who talk too much; *nags*, *scolds*, *scandal-mongers*, *shrews*, *fishwives*, *battle-axes*, *viragos*, *fussers*, *mischief makers*, and plain *old cats* who make life miserable for everyone else by saying what should not be said.

A number of recent studies demonstrate that this pervasive stereotype of women as talkers is a gross caricature and that in conversational interaction between men and women, far from men never being able to get a word in edgeways, they usually have the upper hand. Topics

See Fishman (1978); Maltz and Borker (1982); Spender (1980b); West and Zimmerman (1977); Zimmerman and West (1975).

are determined by, or in deference to, men—by men interrupting, or talking over women in order to get the floor if women do not automatically yield the right by 'asking him about himself and his interests' (advice given to generations of adolescent girls and young women by women's magazines, mothers, and psychologists concerned for the fragile ego of the male that constantly needs boosting by 'making him feel important'!). A graphic instance is provided in Text 2.1, an example cited by West and Zimmerman (1977).

Such behaviour can clearly be seen as dominance display on the part of males, and is by no means always submitted to without protest by females (West, 1979). Behind such displays would seem to lie evaluations of both female and male topic choices and of the point or purpose of different kinds of interaction, that is their nature as genres, that are widely shared by males and females.

The question of 'men's' and 'women's' topics will be taken up again in Chapter 3. For the moment I will merely point out that the response of some males to what they would designate 'women's talk' topics can range from verbally deriding such choices (as 'trivial', 'a waste of time', 'not serious', 'subjective', 'emotional', etc.), to refusing to participate in any discussion involving feelings (even when there is an evident problem in a relationship between a male and a female), to the extreme response of getting up and walking out of the room if certain topics are mentioned.

See the section 'Lexical resources: *woman* and *man*' in Chapter 3, pp. 50–4.

See Schulz (1975); Miller & Swift (1977), Chapter 4.

Such behaviour is obviously important in reinforcing the negative self-image many women have of themselves and in socialising girls and boys from a very early age into such negative evaluations of women and women's talk. This kind of marginalising of women is much less overt than explicit denigration, and is all the more insidious for that. It is not impossible to discern misogyny in insulting words, even when one has heard them used to, and about, women all one's life, because there are also non-pejorative words for women (despite the persistent pattern of pejoration in English). It is very much harder to perceive the

Text 2.1   A conversational interaction between a man and a woman

Woman: How's your paper coming?=

Man: Alright I guess (#) I haven't done much in the past two weeks

  (1.8)

Woman: Yeah:::know how that ⌈ can ⌉

Man: ⌊ Hey ⌋ ya' got an extra cigarette?

  (#)

Woman: Oh uh sure ((hands him the pack)) like **my** ⌈ pa— ⌉

Man: ⌊ How ⌋ 'bout a match?

  (1.2)

Woman: Ere ya go uh like **my** ⌈ pa— ⌉

Man: ⌊ Thanks ⌋

  (1.8)

Woman: Sure (#) I was gonna tell you ⌈ my— ⌉

Man: ⌊ Hey ⌋ I'd really like ta' talk but I gotta run (#) see ya

  (3.2)

Woman: Yeah

Note: an equal sign = indicates no time elapses between contiguous utterances
a hash sign # indicates a pause of one second or less
numbers in parenthesis (1.8) indicate the time in seconds ensuing between speakers' turns
colons ::: indicate that the immediately prior symbol is prolonged
square brackets [] indicate overlapping portions of utterances, i.e. interruptions of the woman by the man
double parenthesis (( )) enclose descriptions, not transcribed utterances
a dash — at the end of a word indicates that the utterance is cut short at that point
Source: West & Zimmerman (1977), pp. 527-8

methods of marginalisation when they are not coded linguistically but only manifested by actions, or rather, a crucial non-action, that of refusing to listen, which can only condemn the would-be speaker to silence. This point, bitterly ironic in the face of the stereotype of the empty-headed female who never stops talking, has not been lost on many contemporary feminist writers. American poet Adrienne Rich, for instance, in a book of essays titled *On Lies, Secrets and Silence* speaks of 'the suffocating silence and denial' that lesbians have met historically, seeing this silence as part of a strategy to obliterate all knowledge of them, and 'part of the totality of silence about women's lives' (Rich, 1979, p. 224).

When one turns, however, from considering what is (and is not) part of the content of conversational interaction as well as attitudes towards that content, to investigating the nature of the social process being enacted through conversation, then it would seem that males and females use conversation differently. Maltz and Borker (1982) summarise a mass of empirical data on differences between male and female talk, by both children and adults. The evidence indicates that while women use conversation primarily for 'negotiating and expressing a relationship', i.e. interactionally, men use conversation as display. Thus joke telling, boasting, ribbing, and other forms of ritualised verbal aggression in which one is expected to be able to 'perform' verbally, to one-up someone else and earn admiration from those observing, are commonly

See Heath (1983) and Labov (1972a) on verbal contests among American Blacks.

found in informal male conversation. For males, getting and holding the floor is of prime importance, while for females 'getting the floor is not seen as particularly problematic . . . What is problematic is getting people engaged and keeping them engaged—maintaining the conversation and the interaction' (Maltz & Borker, 1982, p. 209).

The consequences of such differences are enormous. Maltz and Borker focus on male–female miscommunication, pointing out that differences in verbal strategies and different interpretations of the same strategies lead to misunderstanding and misinterpretation. Their analysis, in terms of males and females belonging to different sociolinguistic subcultures is inadequate, however, in that it goes no further than the question of difference. The question of who benefits from such difference is never asked, but needs to be.

Women seem to be the obvious losers in that their conversational goals and strategies are consistently devalued by males and in that in interaction with males they regularly suffer the indignities of being talked over and at (even sometimes when talking about their own areas of expertise) and having their use of talk to explore issues, personalities, and decision making reinterpreted as requests for instant problem solving. In developmental terms, learning to interact co-operatively will undoubtedly make you more responsive to the cues provided by others about their needs and more able to manage the giving of such cues to others, but that is hardly the kind of verbal skill needed to function successfully as a union advocate, on the courtroom floor, in the lecture theatre, as a politician, sports commentator, chairman of the board of directors—positions of power and influence in our society. If women do succeed in these positions, which involves mastering the kind of talk that is necessary to do the job, then the final touch is that their 'womanliness' or 'femininity' is called into question by the very fact of that mastery: 'real' women don't talk like that.

If one values co-operative talk, however, then men who only participate in 'performance' talk are the losers: if one never learns to use talk as a means of presenting one's self and of responding to others, then one's awareness of self and of others will be that much less precise, less defined, because it has been less articulated. Practising an invulnerable public persona is a dangerous game, then, for little boys: it may end up being the only one they have. But some of them do get to play politicians, union leaders, media magnates, millionaire land-developers, and that must be pretty exciting and some compensation for what they've missed out on. For those who don't quite make it at that level, well, there's always the satisfaction of telling the wife that she doesn't know what she's talking about.

The world of school

The family is the first major social institution that all but a few children experience. School is the second. Both these institutions, as they are experienced by children, have profound effects on their gender identities. Oakley (1972, p.177) notes that 'a multitude of studies agree that by the age of four children have a firm knowledge of sex identity and

28

are well able to perceive distinctions of gender role'. Children bring this knowledge with them into school, which, like the family, is a social institution whose available roles, activities, and goals have been shaped by a social order in which the sexual division of labour is vital to its functioning and which legitimates the consequent inequality between women and men by means of ideology.

Three aspects of school will be investigated in this section. The first issue is the question of the teachers themselves, the genres they use, and the status of the knowledge they deal with, in relation to gender. The second issue is the question of classroom interaction and what it reveals about cultural assumptions of differences between girls and boys and about reinforcement of those differences. The third issue is the question of what children write (genre) and what they write about (field and tenor) as they master the productive side of the new mode, writing, that it is the primary task of the infants' and primary school to teach.

Teachers, teaching, knowledge, and gender

As one progresses up the education hierarchy from kindergarten to university the following observations can be made:

1. A steadily decreasing number of teachers are women. Women have virtually exclusive control of kindergarten and infants' classes, predominate in junior primary classes (but seem to take a smaller proportion of fifth and especially sixth grade classes than their numbers in relation to males would predict), are present in significant numbers in junior secondary classes, but considerably less likely than men to be taking Year 12 classes (other than English), are relatively common as tutors at universities, but less and less common as one proceeds up the academic hierarchy from lecturer to senior lecturer to professor. Currently only 2.1 per cent of professors in Australia are women (Cass et al., 1983).
2. Specialisation of knowledge steadily increases and specialised knowledge is considerably more prestigious than the generalist knowledge of the average infants' or primary teacher.
3. The preferred mode choice for teachers steadily shifts from dialogue to monologue, the lecture providing an opportunity for uninterrupted display of expertise, the focus being on knowledge as thing (as commodity or property, vested in individuals) rather than on knowing/learning as an ongoing process achieved co-operatively.
4. Though the relationship of teacher to students remains one of more powerful to less powerful, the basis of the teacher's power shifts from authority to expertise, i.e. comes to be based on knowledge rather than control. It should also be noted that knowledge itself is by no means neutral in relation to gender. Kagan notes that 'there are strong semantic associations between the dimensions of "masculinity" and "femininity" and specific areas of knowledge for most adult members of western culture' (Kagan, 1965, p. 558, cited by Sears & Feldman, 1966/1974, p.158).

See the section 'Field' in Chapter 4, pp. 56–7.

If one now turns to the question of genre in the classroom, there is undoubtedly continuity between what goes on in the kindergarten

in the way outlined
under points 1—4.

classroom and what happens in both the university tutorial and lecture. What is probably involved is a set of closely related teaching or instruction genres rather than a single genre, however. Teaching at these different levels differs in terms of specific field, tenor, and mode choices, which strongly suggests genre difference, since Martin sees elements of the schematic structure of genre as 'determining particular values of field, mode and tenor' (Martin, 1985b). Such a set of teaching genres is also clearly related at a more general level in terms of the goal of the social process enacted by teachers when teaching. The goal of all teaching would seem to involve the administration of rites of passage that have to be successfully negotiated by students if they are to enter into the adult world with particular degrees of standing. The minimum degree of initial standing is achieved with basic literacy and the maximum with something like a university degree in a highly competitive and prestigious field such as medicine.

Returning now to the initial observation of this section—that the proportion of women teachers to men steadily decreases as one moves up the educational hierarchy—the interconnections between gender, knowledge, mode choice, and kinds of power are suggestive. Firstly, the predominance of males at levels where the lecture is likely to be the preferred mode choice would seem not unrelated to cultural pressures on males to develop skills with display or performance genres. Secondly there seems to be a set of connections between specialised knowledge, high status knowledge, and masculine knowledge, legitimating men as the most appropriate possessors of such knowledge—even including, as long as it is specialised enough, such 'feminine' areas as English literature. This raises a third issue, which is whether any legitimate areas of knowledge/control exist for women.

See the section 'The
world of home and
informal interaction'
above, pp. 24—8.

This point is
elaborated more
fully in the section
'Pronouns' in
Chapter 3, pp.
43—50.

Clearly, control of children is one such legitimated area of power for women (though note that in both family and school, the ultimate authority figure is commonly male—the Father and the Principal). Women's control of children, especially young children, in school is something of a two-edged sword, however—as it can be in the family, where mothers are held responsible for everything that goes wrong with their children. Massing together young humans of the same chronological age in the charge of a single adult is no doubt cost-effective in economic terms, and, if children were the sweet, innocent, biddable creatures that the romantic cult of the child tells us they are, then no doubt teaching would be as easy as many people choose to think it is. The conditions under which much, perhaps most, teaching takes place ensures, however, that the question of control is, and will remain, a central issue, particularly acute during the years of compulsory schooling when women teachers far outnumber men.

Women are doubly disadvantaged as authority figures, and bear a double burden as a consequence. Culturally, women are not seen as authority figures (even their control of children being commonly subject to higher male authority) and the patterns of interaction they are socialised into are fundamentally co-operative, rather than coercive, and do not generally lead to the mastery of genres such as the narrative and the joke, which can be used enormously successfully by males who have mastered them as an alternative to explicit coercive control in the class-

30

room. The constant exercise of coercive control is psychologically stressful (hence the discharge of accumulated affect in those conversations between teachers in which everybody says how awful everything is: the kids, the administration, the financing authorities, the buildings, the parents. . .).

Women not only bear the brunt of this psychological stress (in purely numerical terms if nothing else) but also the opprobrium heaped on them because of the truly terrible things that do happen to children in schools. Everyone has memories of sarcastic, aggressive, spiteful, browbeating teachers, especially from one's more impressionable earlier years at school. For many, the negative attitudes generated by such experiences are generalised not merely to teachers but to women (thereby fuelling ideological convictions that women can't handle power and therefore should never be given any), and are less often seen as deriving from the nature and organisation of the institution of school itself, much less the ideologies that sustain it.

None of this is in any way to deny that much caring co-operative interaction does go on between teachers, both men and women, and students, as individuals and in groups in the classroom. Such interaction would seem to occur despite the inherently coercive nature of the institution itself. The fact that it is found at all, however, is one indication of the potential for adjusting genres (if not, in this case, inventing a totally new one) in the face of ideologically derived institutional shapings of social process that are implicitly or explicitly seen as unacceptable.

Teacher–student talk in the classroom

Let us now turn our attention to the student in the (mixed sex) classroom and ask the following questions: Who talks to the teacher? Who gets talked to by the teacher? What kinds of talk are involved (and how are these evaluated)? What are the consequences of classroom interaction in relation to gender?

The answer to the first two questions (who talks and who gets talked to) is boys predominantly. The stereotype would have it that women talk more than men, and the superior verbal fluency of girls has been an article of faith among psychologists for many years (see Cherry, 1975b, p. 175), contributing in no small way to the widespread conviction among teachers that girls are better at language as a core component of the curriculum; but the evidence is clear that in mixed classes girls do not talk as much as boys.

Sears and Feldman summarise the findings of one large-scale study of 21 fourth and sixth grade classes in the following terms:

> Teachers interacted more with boys than with girls on every one of the four major categories of teaching behavior: approval, instruction, listening to the child, and disapproval. Thus it appears that boys receive more of the teacher's active attention than girls do.
> (Sears & Feldman, 1966/1974, p. 149)

Boys are generally more aggressive than girls and 'more disruptive and noncompliant', particularly in the pre-school classroom (Cherry, 1975b, pp. 180, 175), so that higher levels of disapproval of boys are to some extent predictable, particularly in relation to rule violation. Other studies confirm these findings as far as levels of both disapproval and approval of boys are concerned.

See Sears & Feldman (1966/1974, pp. 149–51) for references and outlines of findings.

Fichtelius et al. (1980), looking more closely at the linguistic form of teacher questions addressed to children aged from three to seven in individual interaction, found that more open-ended questions were directed to boys and more yes/no questions, to girls. (This study involved Swedish-speaking children, but the cultural continuity between all Western societies suggests that similar findings would appear in a study of English-speaking children.)

The consequences of such teacher practices would seem to be very positive for boys. Fichtelius et al. suggest that:

> Through the mode of questioning employed, the older boys are allowed, more than girls, to develop their verbal abilities as well as their power of self-motivation and imagination.
>
> (Fichtelius et al., 1980, p. 224)

Sears and Feldman see similar outcomes for boys, but disturbingly negative ones for girls, as they ask:

> What should we expect the social learnings of boys and girls to be as they go through many hours of interaction with teachers during their elementary school years? One consequence might be a cumulative increase in independent, autonomous behavior by boys as they are disapproved, praised, listened to and taught more actively by the teacher. Another might be a lowering of self-esteem generally for girls as they receive less attention and are criticized more for their lack of knowledge and skill.
>
> (Sears & Feldman, 1966/1974, p. 150)

The last point refers to Spaulding's finding that 40 per cent of the disapproval of girls was for lack of knowledge or skill as against only 26 per cent of total disapproval of the boys for this reason.

Males undoubtedly do 'develop their verbal abilities' and display 'independent, autonomous behaviour' in classrooms from primary school to the post-graduate classroom. Sears and Feldman note that 'boys in upper-elementary grades participate more than girls do in classroom discussion, making more statements and asking more questions' (Sears & Feldman, 1966/1974, p. 149). At the secondary level, Elliot (1974) found minimal participation from the girls in his fourth-year class on a War and Society project, which seemed due to the topic itself, which was 'viewed as the territorial preserve of the boys' (in Sarah, 1980, p. 161) and also to the fact that 'the girls were threatened by being required to talk to boys' (Spender, 1980a, p. 150). Talking in class, particularly on a 'male' topic, had come to be seen as a male prerogative. Spender notes Elliot's conclusion that he 'was forcing the girl students to play an "unfeminine" role when he insisted that they take part in classroom discussion with boys' (Spender, 1980a, p. 150).

Parker (1973) found that male undergraduates talked significantly more often than their female counterparts in the discussion sections of introductory courses in history and sociology and that

32

both sexes regarded talking in class, particularly in the form of questioning or challenging, as specifically masculine behaviour, and no doubt the same would apply to most teachers as to students. It was perfectly proper that boys should conduct arguments, air their views and query information, but it was not at all proper for girls to do the same thing.

(Spender, 1980a, p. 150)

Even at the post-graduate level, males are twice as likely as females to ask a question during a lecture and are more likely to ask a question going beyond the text of the lecture, while women are more likely to ask a question relating directly to the text of the lecture (Packham, 1982).

Spender is quite explicit about the consequences of female silence in school:

Female silence is exploited by educational institutions and contributes to the over-representation of males and the under-representation of females in those who achieve educational success.

(Spender, 1980a, p. 149)

The precise mechanism of such female disadvantaging will involve the lack of opportunity for girls to talk their way into learning, to 'talk knowledge into place' (Barnes, 1976) and the progressive alienation of girls from school because 'their interests do not need to be accommodated' (Spender, 1980a, p. 152). Boys' interests **must** be taken into account in choosing reading materials, themes or topics within subject areas, and even the content of text books, because boys will not tolerate 'girls' topics' but girls will not actively protest at 'boys' topics'.

If the education system by and large fails to accommodate female interests and topics, either because certain fields are designated as masculine or by the 'masculinising' of feminine fields such as English and history, then three options are available to women: opt out as soon as possible (still the choice of many able young women), attempt to beat the males at their own game (remembering that if they succeed, as many women have succeeded, the costs will almost certainly include a questioning of their feminine credentials (by others if not also by the women themselves), and/or a lack of solidarity with ordinary women, who are 'boring' while men are 'much more interesting'). The third option is one that has much more recently become available, or rather is still in the process of being worked out. It involves women learning about themselves and other women through women's studies courses, thus providing real opportunities to talk, learn, and know as women and to begin to think about what they want to achieve and on what terms they want to achieve it. Conklin suggests that women have the option of developing new genres as one way of 'establishing their credentials' in the public domain: '[Women] must recognize, legitimize, and creatively develop their own speech genres' (Conklin, 1974, quoted in Thorne & Henley, 1975b, p. 257).

Just as radical, but in a somewhat different way, is Spender's advocacy of changes in the style of men's talk:

It is vitally important for women to start to talk but it is not necessary that we emulate the habits of men. Research has indicated that although men talk more, they exert more control over talk, and that they interrupt more (Zimmerman and West, 1975). Women listen more, are more supportive when they do talk (Hirschman, 1973, 1974) and have greater expertise in terms of sustaining conversations (Fishman, 1975). It is precisely these qualities which have been neither valued nor acknowledged. Rather than women learning to talk like men it would seem to be preferable if men were to learn to listen more and to be more supportive of the conversation of others. This could revolutionise our patterns of talk in society, and a vast range of oppressive images, of both men and women, will be undermined.

(Spender, 1980a, p. 154)

Such a change would revolutionise more than patterns of talk and relations between men and women: if it were to be effected it would necessitate discarding traditional and totally unquestioned ways of thinking about knowledge and ways of knowing and about the relationship of humanity to the natural and social worlds it inhabits. In other words, not merely educational institutions would be irrevocably changed but the whole basis of Western capitalist society with its values of individualism, ownership, and control. The generic repertoire of a culture, its ways of speaking, arises out of the particular ways that being, knowing, and acting are conceived as possible within that culture. To propose to change ways of speaking, then, is to propose changing the culture in a far more profound way than could conceivably be achieved by changes to the vocabulary of a language.

Genre has mostly been implicit rather than explicit in this discussion of teacher−student talk, mainly because appropriate linguistically informed empirical work has yet to be done. The next section, dealing with children's writing, will focus on genre very explicitly and attempt to make links between what children write and what they say in class with respect to the question of the terms on which girls and boys are allowed to find out about and participate in the world they live in.

Children writing

Boys may talk in class, and be approved for it insofar as certain kinds of classroom talk are seen as essentially masculine activities. Girls write. And as a group they generally do it better than boys, though the really outstanding writers in a class or school may be male (as was the case in the large-scale study of writing in a Sydney primary school now in progress under the direction of J.R. Martin at the University of Sydney). Boys and girls differ in what they write (genre) and what they write about (field), and it is the nature of these differences, their sources, and their implications that will be the focus of attention in this section.

See Martin (1984) and Martin & Rothery (1984).

Girls and boys write about different things almost from the start, with the difference increasing with age and the common ground becoming smaller. Girls write about home activities (including relationships between family members), dress and appearance, romance, and fantasy worlds inhabited by fairies, witches, characters from children's stories (e.g. Mr Men and Little Miss), commercial toys (e.g. Strawberry Shortcake), and talking animals and objects. Boys write about playing or watching sport and other physical activities such as bike-riding. ('My BMX Bike'—either the one I have or the one I'd like to have—was probably the single most frequent topic for boys from kindergarten to Grade 6 in the primary school study referred to above.) Boys' fantasy worlds are inhabited by creatures from outer space, assorted monsters (preferably of the kind that kill people unexpectedly and messily, with lots of blood), everyday burglars, kidnappers, and murderers—and when the writer himself is a character in an adventure story then he is usually accompanied by a group of his male class-mates. 'The Day My Friends and I Went to Cairo', written by a Year 6 boy, names no less than seven boys accompanying the writer on this adventure (Martin, 1984). Boys also write about topics that do not lend themselves to 'story'-writing e.g. the solar system, dinosaurs, radios. And this last fact is immensely significant as far as genre choice is concerned.

In the very early stages of learning to write, the predominant genres employed by both girls and boys are identified by Martin and Rothery (1984) as:

1. Picture Description (description of a picture including exophoric demonstrative):

   This is a tadpole almost lost its tail. (Year 1)

2. Observation/Comment (specific observations and optional expression of attitude):

   The Park
   One Sunday morning I went to play football and we had to play Woodlands.
   I am number five.
   I am hooker next I am playing five-eight.
   I had to go off the field because I got kicked in the stomach.
   My coach was sad and that was the End. (Year 2)

By the time children move from the infants' school to the primary school they are writing substantial numbers of Recounts. This is the predominant genre of the infants' school.

3. Recount (temporal sequence of events without a crisis):

   Our trip to Liverpool Library
   We went to Liverpool Library very happily. We walked there. We sat down and listened to Miss Matthews. Then after she had finished we filled in a few questions about where things are in the library. We saw a film about a tailor who killed seven flies in one blow. It was fun. (Year 3)

The Recount is the predominant genre in the primary years, with Narrative (temporal sequence of events with Complication/Resolution Structure) becoming more common in Years 5 and 6. The other genre that can first appear in the infants' school but becomes significant in the primary years is the Report. Other than when this genre is specifically required by the teacher as part of class-work, boys produce many more Reports than girls when asked simply to write.

4. Report (descriptions, usually of generic participants):

   Birds
   Birds live up in a tree. If they don't eat they die. Redbirds blackbirds any coloured birds Dark birds light birds. Some are small and others are big. (Year 3)

Within the context of the primary school, the most highly valued genre is Narrative, in particular the narrative of vicarious experience (Rothery, 1980). Girls rather than boys produce the most highly valued texts of this kind. What distinguishes the girls' from the boys' texts is that girls produce single Complication^Resolution structures, where boys have a preference for repetitive (serial) structures, which girls almost never produce; and girls write about topics that their teachers can approve of, while boys' topics can and do upset teachers, leading in some cases to banning of certain topic choices. The serial form itself may also be banned in an attempt to force the boys to give their narratives what the teachers regard as a more satisfactory shape.

On the face of it, the banning response to boys' choice of the content and generic structure of their narratives looks like sexist discrimination against males, and Martin goes so far as to suggest that such behaviour directed against males 'tends to push them away from an interest in literature and languages in general and into more scientifically oriented courses in later years' (Martin, 1985a). In fact it may well be the case that it is precisely because many boys are already oriented towards masculine fields, including science, that they choose the topics they do—in part to assert their maleness against girls' 'poofy' writing (one boy's characterisation at an Open Day display, which nicely captures the superiority and derision of many boys in the face of girls' writing), in part maintaining continuity with the autonomous, independent talk noted above, and in part rejecting the ideological expectations of teachers that children should be innocent, biddable, ignorant of death, destruction, and human misery, and generally unwise in the ways of the world.

Girls in their writing demonstrate that they are children, thereby earning the approval of their teachers, while boys are boys and, as such, are suspect and troublesome in this ideological world. But the world of primary school is of limited duration: beyond it is the world of secondary school and beyond that again, the adult world of work and leisure. Boys may find primary school boring, even actively unpleasant at times (though hardly all the time), but their refusal to be confined to the world of childhood gives them an inestimable advantage over girls in a real world where knowing about things and how they work, knowing something about how to manipulate people to react in ways you want them to, being able to voice an objection, develop an argument, ridicule an opponent, entertain one's friends with irreverence and humour all count in terms of achieving and maintaining a place in that real world. Telling fairy stories, even telling good fairy stories very well, for all that has been said about the importance of fantasy in psychological development, simply doesn't count. The positions of real power and influence in our society necessitate command of genres for which boys' educational experience provides an appropriate preparation and girls' doesn't. Even in terms of the written genre of most significance in secondary and most tertiary education—Exposition (explanations provided in support of a generalisation)—girls' genre competence at primary school is not merely irrelevant but positively disabling.

See Martin (1989).

By being socialised into living out adults' ideological expectations of childhood, girls are marginalised from their earliest years. That marginalisation effectively excludes most girls from developing the same

36

levels of competence as boys in the ways our culture has developed for knowing about and acting in the real world. Teachers could do much, by selectively and sensitively directing the genre and field selections of girls and boys, to ensure that all children gain experience with a range of ways of meaning they might otherwise ignore, if left to their own devices. Before teachers can be in a position to begin to do this, however, we need to know much more about genre both in and out of the classroom. Such work is really only beginning.

Home and school as preparation for what?

It is not hard to demonstrate that, in probabilistic terms, men and women as groups command different genre repertoires: certain genres are more likely to have been acquired by individuals of one gender than the other. This fact has been used to argue for innate differences between females and males on the basis of a somewhat naive notion of choice: men and women do act differently, therefore they must be choosing to act differently, thereby revealing their inner, 'real' difference. And because genres are on the whole not visible in terms of their schematic structures but are seen as some kind of holistic emanation of individual cognitive ability rather than as staged social processes that have to be learned, then mastery of culturally valued genres is seen as an indication of intellectual superiority and failure to master them is proof of inferiority.

Precisely the same logic applies to genre and class, especially in relation to learning to write.

The two previous sections, on the worlds of home and school, have outlined the case for seeing the home and the school as selectively encouraging or discouraging genre learning regarded as appropriate or inappropriate in relation to gender. Such selective opportunity to learn genres, beginning in very early childhood, is important not only in itself, in terms of primary genres mastered or not mastered, but in terms of the extent to which the skills and orientations learned early underlie the genre options of adult life. What is learned early is the basis for the adult genre repertoire that is potentially available, i.e. for what the individual can say and do, and hence for the individual conception of self.

Perhaps the clearest instance so far in the literature of selective socialisation into genre, with all its consequences for later social roles and self-perception, is Heath's (1983) account of infant boys in the Black community she calls Trackton being taught how to stand up for themselves verbally and, in the process of learning certain verbal skills in mastering a culturally-valued genre, coming to define themselves as certain kinds of people (Heath, 1983, ch.3). It is surely significant, however, that this account is of the learning of a genre that is not found in White society—the 'exotic' is visible whereas what is fundamental to one's own society remains largely invisible. There is urgent need then for a range of detailed ethnographic studies of the kind undertaken by Heath, informed by the richest kind of linguistic theory about how meanings are made and used in different social groups (including our own) and how children learn those meanings.

See Heath (1983), Chapter 3.

Despite the fact of different genre repertoires for men and women, there has been increasing overlap as barriers to women's admission to

37

various social roles, especially in paid employment, have been broken down: some (though not many) women work as industrial advocates, airline pilots, skilled tradespeople, political journalists, and municipal council gardeners, and all these roles will necessitate the learning of appropriate genres. Blocking access to social role and hence social process is now widely seen as blatantly discriminatory and unacceptable, though there are still ideological die-hards who want to keep women out of certain roles and in their proper place. (In industrial contexts, blocking of access has often taken the form of refusing the admission of women to factories and job-sites on the grounds that there are no separate toilet facilities for them. This at least is true, if specious, unlike one of the nineteenth-century arguments used to refuse women access to higher education, which was that their ovaries would wither. Many Victorian mothers of large families might well have regretted the unavailability of such a boon.)

That totally blocking access is no longer socially acceptable does not mean that women (and men) who want to move out of traditional roles have it easy. They frequently have to cope with their sexual identity being impugned (no real woman would ever want to drive a semi-trailer; kindergarten teaching is not a job for a real man). And women find that they do have to be better than their male colleagues in order to make it at all because women's performance is consistently evaluated as inferior to men's. A sobering experimental demonstration of this, showing how women have learned only too well that men do and say it better (whatever it is), is found in Goldberg's study of responses to identical pieces of writing, from various fields, ascribed to either a male or a female author (Goldberg, 1968/1974). Out of a total of 54 possible comparisons, Goldberg found that 'three were tied, seven favoured the female authors—and the number favoring the male authors was 44!' (p. 41). The fields from which the pieces of writing were drawn were selected on the basis of a pre-test, which asked students from the same population to rate 'the degree to which you associate the field with men or with women' (p. 39). Two 'male' fields (law and city-planning), two 'female' fields (elementary-school teaching and dietetics), and two 'neutral' fields, not strongly associated with either sex (linguistics and art history) were selected. Articles assumed to be written by males were rated higher than those thought to be written by females in all fields, the differences being statistically significant for city-planning, linguistics, and especially law.

Since all Goldberg's subjects were female college students, he sees his findings as demonstrating that 'women seem to think that men are better at everything—including elementary-school teaching and dietetics' (p. 40). It would seem that these women had learned only too well that the genres appropriate for professional discussion were not for them. And hardly surprisingly when teachers discount girls' competence and

> classify it as not genuine ability. When boys ask the right questions, it shows that they are bright; when girls ask them it shows they know what is expected of them.
>
> (Spender, 1980a, p. 152)

Women as linguistic performers are consistently downgraded by men as well as women; women's talk is *gossip* or *chat*, while men's is *discussion*; women novelists write *women's novels*, about women and men that are not universal, while men novelists write *novels*, about men and women that are; women speaking or writing with passion about controversial issues are *shrill* and *hysterical*, epithets seldom applied to men simply because one disagrees with them. But even in the face of incontrovertible evidence of inadequate linguistic performance on the part of those many men with poor social skills, the ones who have difficulty with face-to-face conversation, much less a telephone conversation or a personal letter, the worst that will usually be said is simply that they are socially incompetent—and worse things can be said of a man than that you can't hold a conversation with him. Many men who experience this kind of difficulty are, of course, keenly aware of it as a problem, and value the interpersonal skills that women learn as part of their socialisation but which they, as males, had limited access to. Such men may even succeed in extending their linguistic competence, thereby making possible new kinds of valued relationships.

This expansion of male generic competence into traditionally 'female' territory, an expansion that is happening with greater frequency and is valued by women, highlights the fact that men's area of legitimate social functioning is larger than that of women and may more legitimately extend into the traditionally 'female' areas than vice versa. There seems greater social acceptance of male nurses than female motor mechanics, for instance. The expectation that women will be actively involved in only some of the major social institutions and marginally involved, if at all, in others (e.g. family and school compared with banking and industrial relations) means that women are linguistically prepared for only a restricted range of social processes and thereby denied the possibility of organising discourse to achieve the full range of culturally validated goals. Male socialisation into genre is selective too, but since males are socially defined as competent, they are less likely to feel powerless, inadequate, or unable to achieve desired goals without access to 'female' genres than women feel with respect to 'male' genres. And where a lack is felt, leading to the attempt to acquire 'female' genres, then such learning is likely to be seen as extension of the male preserve rather than trespass on the female preserve, unlike the situation of the woman learning a 'male' genre, who is made very conscious that she is an intruder.

One further kind of genre needs to be identified that is certainly produced by both men and women but is of particular interest because it directly enacts the ideology of gender as characterised in the section 'Male versus female' above in what it says about men and women and their relationships. Such genres include the Pornographic Story, the Dirty Joke, and the Romance as purveyed by publishing firms such as Mills and Boon.

See pp. 17–20.

Analysis of the schematic structure of such ideologically revealing genres, firstly in terms of the register choices through which the elements of structure are manifested, and then through the linguistic choices that in turn realise those register choices, should reveal in exaggerated form the patterns that are identifiable in less concentrated, repetitive and hence

See Faust (1980) on pornography, including the sub-genre on romances referred to in the trade as bodice-rippers, in Chapter

13; Legman (1972) on dirty jokes; and Thwaite (1983) for the linguistic analysis of those Mills & Boon romances, using the same systemic model as is being used here, with the focus on lexico-grammar. Some of her findings will be discussed below.

explicit form in much everyday discourse—from advertising jingles to job interviews to everyday conversation. Or, to start from the other end, the actual language of texts—how they are constituted as texts, what words and wordings are used and, to a lesser extent, how this linguistic content is realised in linguistic form as sounds on the air-waves or marks on paper—is constrained by the realities of the institutions men and women are, and may legitimately be, involved in, the kinds of social relationships they do, and may legitimately, have with others, and the modes of communication they do, and may legitimately, employ. It is to these questions we now turn.

Chapter 3

Lexis and gender

Introduction

In focusing attention, in this and subsequent chapters, on the semiotic planes of language and register in relation to gender, I will begin in this chapter with lexis, with words. The discussion will include some of the lexical issues familiar from critiques of the English language as sexist, such as personal titles (*Ms*, *Mrs*, *Miss*) and the use of the pronoun *he* as a supposedly generic pronoun.

The intention will be to explore the extent to which the lexical resources of the English language are systematically distorted by the ideology of gender. Such distortion may take a variety of forms, including different evaluative loadings on lexis referring to women and to men and the proliferation of lexis referring to one or other gender in particular ways (for women, lexis referring to them pejoratively, especially in sexual terms, proliferates). Or such distortion may be reflected in prescriptive rules about pronoun use.

In English, the distorting effects of gender ideology on language as resource, as system, are most visible and blatant in lexis. This is why lexis has received so much attention from those concerned with sexist language. But as we shall see, grammar does not remain unaffected by sexist ideology, nor is it the case that the way women and men learn to make use of the resources of phonology and discourse are unaffected by ideological considerations.

Personal titles

Let us begin with the question of personal titles, one of the small number of issues involving language and gender that has been widely discussed and where public awareness (though not always understanding) is high. Until recently the English personal title system consisted of three terms: *Miss* or *Mrs* referring to women, the choice depending on their marital status, and *Mr* for men, regardless of their marital status. (At various times in the past, other terms have been part of the system, e.g. *Master* for males and *Mistress* for females. Note that both *Mrs* and *Miss* are derived from the older title *Mistress*.) The set of contemporary choices can be represented as in Figure 3.1. This system network makes very clear that in choosing titles in English two pieces of information are needed to make a correct choice for women (gender and marital status) but only one for men (gender).

Figure 3.1

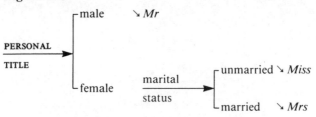

Poynton (1981, pp. 14–17) details such gender asymmetries for various forms of address.

The lack of parallelism is noteworthy in itself, though not at all uncharacteristic of systems involving gender. The basis of the asymmetry is that while males are identified purely in terms of gender, females are distinguished in terms of their relationship to a male: either as daughter of one—since children usually (and in some places compulsorily) take their father's surname—or as wife of another. Hence the proposal to introduce a new term *Ms*, which would parallel *Mr* in simply identifying the referent as female without reference to marital status. There have been suggestions to do away with even that distinction, e.g. a universal *M* whenever a title is required for the sake of politeness or formality, but distinguishing people on the basis of sex/gender is so fundamental in this culture that it is doubtful that such a change would ever occur. *Ms* is a somewhat different matter, however, though the current situation regarding its use is not quite what was envisaged, which can be represented as in Figure 3.2.

Figure 3.2

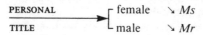

What seems to have happened instead is that the new item has been assimilated into the old system for women, demonstrating that it is one thing to suggest changing a system (by adding or subtracting a term) but quite another to propose to abolish one: it is easier to add new meanings or change old ones than to simply make meanings disappear.

One possible response to Ms, particularly by those who know nothing about the term other than that it refers to women, is to attempt to incorporate it in the original network (Figure 3.1) as in Figure 3.3.

Figure 3.3

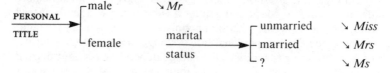

The question mark stands for various actual interpretations of *Ms*, as referring to a woman living in a *de facto* relationship, or a divorced woman, or a lesbian, i.e. still defining women in terms of marital status, but extending the traditional set of options. For many people, however, *Ms* has the much more specific meaning of feminist, so that for them the network representing title choices would be as in Figure 3.4.

Figure 3.4

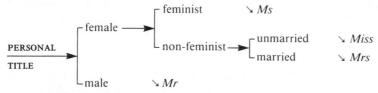

It is interesting to speculate on which of these latter two networks more closely represents the actual distinctions in meaning for the titles for women used by those who have drawn up the various official forms now in use that incorporate all three possible choices.

The nomination of Geraldine Ferraro as Democratic Vice-Presidential candidate for the 1984 Presidential election in the United States apparently led to some soul-searching on the part of journalists and newspapers previously implacably opposed to the use of *Ms*. Ferraro's own preference is for *Ms*, but in the pages of the *New York Times* she was consistently referred to as *Mrs Ferraro*, though Ferraro is her own name and not that of her husband. The newspaper justified itself by saying that 'We accept anyone's choice . . . of a professional name, but a title is not part of the name' (in Peterson, 1984). The linguistic status of titles is not a simple straightforward matter, however (Poynton, in preparation). The *New York Times* would seem to be guilty of arrogance on two counts: categorising a public figure contrary to her expressed wishes (and inaccurately, to boot) and determining a linguistic matter by fiat.

See Miller & Swift (1977, pp. 88–94) on the history of female titles in English and responses to *Ms*; and Vetterling-Braggin (1981) for a number of papers on this issue.

Pronouns

Nearly as familiar in debates about sexist language and language as sexist is the issue of the use of the masculine pronoun (*he, him, his*) when referring to an unspecified or hypothetical individual, in such instances as:

Any attempt to list the qualities of a good manager demonstrates why *he* cannot exist . . .

(cited in Miller & Swift, 1981, p. 37)

Everyone should make up *his* own mind.

. . .every child will develop more quickly or more slowly than 'the average' depending upon the sorts of experiences made available to *him*.

(Edgar et al., 1987, pp. 4-5)

There is, in fact, a series of interrelated issues concerning the selection of singular gender-marked pronouns in English (*she* as well as *he*), which goes well beyond the question of the use of the masculine forms as generic, or linguistically unmarked, i.e. referring to any human being.

Firstly, many languages in the world do not make a gender-based distinction with their third-person singular pronouns, e.g. Finnish, Persian (an Indo-European language, so related, albeit distantly, to English), Yoruban (spoken in Nigeria, which marks status of the referent with respect to the speaker but not gender). As Ordoubadian (1979, p. 420) points out, however, one must not assume a simple relationship between the presence or absence of certain lexical items in a language and attitudes and practices related to gender in the societies that speak those languages. Persian, Azarbayjani, and Yoruban societies are all characterised as considerably more sexist than English-speaking societies, but their languages are less so, lexically. Thus one cannot draw any conclusions from the fact that languages range in their pronoun systems from those that make no gender distinctions, through those that make a distinction for singular referents only (as English), to those that mark gender for both singular and plural (e.g. French). In the latter case, this is related to the grammatical fact that all nouns in the language are marked for (grammatical) gender—and again, there is no basis for assuming that a language that has grammatical gender is more, or less, prone to seeing the world through ideological lenses in relation to gender.

It all depends on how the system is used. Which brings us to the question of the normative rule in English requiring the use of *he* when the referent is unspecified or hypothetical or a representative of a set or class of humans—even when that set is known to include females as well as males or indeed to be entirely female. Many people regard such a rule as an immutable rule of English grammar, not knowing that it is a 'rule' of fairly recent origin, formulated by prescriptive grammarians more concerned with logic, Latin, and, in this case, the preeminence of the male than traditional English ways of using pronouns. Fowler's *Dictionary of Modern English Usage*, more accurately, regards the use of the masculine pronoun 'where the matter of sex is not conspicuous or important' as a convention and identifies both the grammatical origin of the difficulty (the lack of a gender-neutral third person pronoun in English) and a possible social origin of the masculine-as-generic solution in 'an arrogant demand on the part of male England' (Fowler 1965, p. 404).

Early prescriptive grammarians made this abundantly plain, seeing the masculine form as superior to the feminine because men are worthier than women. The 'rule' that the masculine pronoun included the feminine was first formalised in 1746 and in 1850 was enshrined in English law in the *Acts Interpretation Act* 1850 (which also became law in Australia). Between those two dates and well beyond, into the twentieth century, educated practice has by no means always conformed to this convention, and many objections were raised to it in both literary and legal contexts. Furthermore, despite the explicit direction of the Acts Interpretation Act that 'words importing the masculine gender shall be deemed and taken to include females' (Parliament of Victoria, Legal and Constitutional Committee 1983, p.139)—an approach that affected legal documents of all kinds (and helped to spread the convention with the backing of 'the Law')—women were nevertheless excluded. Miller and Swift (1981, pp. 34-5) refer to the move to admit women to the all-male Massachusetts Medical Society in 1879 being defeated on the grounds that the Society's by-laws dealing with membership used *he*. And a woman graduating in law from the University of Sydney in 1902 was unable to practise, until the law was changed sixteen years later, because the original provisions regarding the right to practise applied to all *persons* who had satisfied the appropriate conditions. And in legal definitions going back to the eighteenth century, women are not persons (*University of Sydney News*, 31 July 1984, p.178).

In terms of the consequences of the 'generic *he*' (which goes beyond pronoun choice to the many instances in English of male as norm, as linguistically unmarked), Kramer et al. (1978, p. 644) are quite un-equivocal that it is 'a prime example of the way in which language renders females invisible'. Despite the claims made that the generic masculine includes females, there is a growing body of evidence indicating that this simply is not the case. Writers using generic *man* and *he* slide easily into referring to *the wife* (and other accoutrements and appendages of the male) of the putatively generic manager, executive, or human: school history text-books, for instance, are replete with pioneers who, with their wives and children, moved out of the coastal areas into the real bush (in Australia) or moved West (in the United States). In the following British Rail advertisement, directed at company executives, what might have been generic reference at the beginning is unequivocally male at the end:

On the history of generic *he* see Bodine (1975b) and Parliament of Victoria, Legal and Constitutional Committee (1983).

> Consider the effects long-distance driving can have on an executive. Chances are when he arrives at his meeting he'll be feeling every inch of that journey. Worse, his tiredness may make him unresponsive and irritable. Would **you** feel happy about doing business with a man like that?
>
> (Miller & Swift, 1981, p. 39)

In material written for children, *he* overwhelmingly has actual or implied masculine antecedents (Graham, 1975). It is hardly surprising, then, that in one study school students at both primary and secondary levels, and tertiary students as well, chose more male illustrations for supposedly generic topics like 'urban man' than for such general titles as 'urban life' (Schneider & Hacker, 1973). Kramer et al. suggest that:

> The language development of female children may differ from that of males because of sexist language: a boy, who has heard masculine terms in reference to himself, may more readily accept 'generic' usage than a girl, who must shift her expectations to try to include herself in masculine pronouns. Throughout life women are placed at a special disadvantage because only they 'have the task of making sense of the fact that they are both "man" and "not man" at the same time' (Bate, 1975).
>
> (Kramer et al., 1978, p. 645)

See Kramer et al. (1978, pp. 644–5) for a brief but very useful overview, and Silveira (1980, p. 170) for a more extensive listing of experimental studies.

There is an increasing number of experimental investigations of the generic masculine. For a final word on this subject, consider the following, from a male president of Mills College in the 1950s:

The penetration of this habit of language into the minds of little girls as they grow up to be women is more profound than most people, including most women, have recognized; for it implies that personality is really a male attribute, and that women are a human subspecies.

(Lynn White, cited in Miller & Swift, 1977, p.x)

The findings of Broverman et al. (1972) that mental health professionals see the mentally healthy adult person and the adult male in essentially the same terms, and the mentally healthy adult female in very different terms, should come as no surprise. As the statutes have insisted, women are not persons.

The next issue concerning pronoun choice involves its use in personification, both in everyday conversation and in literature for children. In both cases, the implications are clear for a covert grammatical category of gender. Mathiot with Roberts (1979) investigated deviations from the normative pattern of use of *he* with masculine reference, *she* with feminine reference, and *it* with non-human reference, which were found to be 'much more numerous and varied than is surmised in normative grammars' (Mathiot with Roberts, 1979, p. 3). Examples cited include the following:

Doesn't she look beautiful with her new paint job?

(the referent is a car; the speaker
is a woman, p. 36)

The storm wrecked my whole farm. She spared nothing.

(the speaker is a farmer, p. 38)

You can take her around the corner real quick!

(the referent is a skateboard; the
speaker is a teenage boy, p. 40)

He's so little but cute!

(the referent is a cactus; the
speaker is a woman who calls all
her plants *he*, p. 41)

Will you look at that crazy bird? He's going to break his wings beating them against the window like that!

(the speaker is a woman, p. 41)

Now you take his one end and I will take his other. If we really cooperate we will be able to get him hung up before the store closes.

(the referent is curtains; the speaker
an assistant in the drapery section
of a department store, p. 42)

Mathiot sees her findings as demonstrating 'that Americans hold a complex conception of the nature of entities' that, in what she calls the intimate as distinct from the normative pattern of usage of referential gender, involves including 'their perception of their own social structure in addition to that of their environment' (Mathiot with Roberts 1979, pp. 26, 26-27). In the light of the fact that children are exposed to the intimate pattern of everyday conversational usage from the day they're born, meeting more normative usage later (for many, not until school—and then meeting the overwhelming use of masculine reference demonstrated by Graham (1975) and the pattern of sex-stereotyped personification identified in children's literature by MacKay and Konishi (1980)), it would be surprising if children escaped internalising culturally appropriate stereotypic attitudes to *she* and *he*, male and female.

Tables 3.1 and 3.2 reproduce Tables 8 and 9 of Mathiot's paper, providing a kind of summary, at least in terms of the basic oppositions she sees underlying usage by women and men about male and female.

Table 3.1 The descriptive mode in the intimate pattern

Semantic oppositions corresponding to the formal opposition 'she' vs. 'he'	Basic attributes of women and men	
Beautiful vs. Ugly	Women: beautiful	
	Men: ugly	Men's inherent image
Incompetent vs. Competent	Women: incompetent	
	Men: competent	
Challenge or Reward vs. Brave	Women: a challenge to, or reward for, men	
	Men: brave	
Prized possession vs. Good-Natured	Women: men's prized possessions	
	Men: good natured	
Mature vs. Infantile	Women: mature	Women's inherent image
	Men: infantile	

Source: Mathiot (1979), p. 22

47

Table 3.2 The interpersonal mode in the intimate pattern.

Basic attributes of women and men	Men's self-attributed roles *vis-à-vis* women	Corresponding roles attributed to women	Interpretation
Women: beautiful Men: ugly	Satyr	Nymph	= *Earthbound* ugliness vs. *ethereal* beauty
Women: incompetent Men: competent	Master	Apprentice	= *Intellectual superiority of men over women*
Women: a challenge to, or reward for, men; men's prized possessions	Conqueror	Sex object	= Women as a *prize*
	Owner	Possession	= Women as a *valuable object*

	Men's self-attributed roles *vis-à-vis* men	Corresponding roles attributed to men	
Men: brave, good-natured	Opponent	Opponent	= Relationship based on *mutual esteem*
	Buddy	Buddy	= Relationship based on *trust*

	Women's self-attributed role *vis-à-vis* men	Corresponding role attributed to men	
Women: mature Men: infantile	Mother	Child	= *Emotional superiority of women over men*

Source: Mathiot (1979), p. 23

Two other papers in the same volume, McConnell-Ginet, 1979 and Rudes and Healy, 1979, are related and extremely stimulating. The latter is an investigation of concepts of femaleness and maleness in the (male) gay world, based on the use of *he* and *she*. McConnell-Ginet's paper works towards a semantic analysis of the set of pronouns *he*, *she*, and *they* used with singular antecedents, based on observed usage and elicited judgments of acceptability rather than on normative rules. She concludes her paper in the following terms:

> Pronouns can refer to real people or to fictive prototypes. So long as most of us believe that women and men are what really exist, that androgynes are simply abstract entities, we will tend to sexualise our prototypes as we personalize them. So long as we obey the edicts of prescriptive grammarians and choose *he* for sex-indefinite singular antecedents, we prolong the linguistic and sociocultural invisibility of women.
> (McConnell-Ginet, 1979, p.80)

Finally, let us look at the question of what pronoun choices are available for referring to a single human being. The traditional choices have been either generic *he* (whose continued use cannot be sanctioned, despite all the weight of 'linguistic authority' its proponents invoke) and *they* (the case for which is in fact strong). As well, there are various compound forms, such as *he or she* and *s/he*. Such forms have been devised as a solution to a real problem, but are unlikely to gain wide currency. The former is regarded by many as cumbersome and the latter, while visually very neat in written English (which is why I have chosen to use it in various places in this book), has no spoken form and no comparable object form linking *him* and *her*. Both have the further disadvantage, as many would see it, of drawing attention to the question of gender. One might argue that what is needed is a pronoun form that draws attention away from that issue.

Contemporary purists may wince, but as the Legal and Constitutional Committee of the Victorian Parliament's *Report on the Interpretation Bill 1982*, p.145, points out, '"they" as a singular pronoun has a long and respected history'. The report goes on to identify such major figures of English literature as Jane Austen, Walter Scott, Shakespeare, Addison, Swift, and John Ruskin as all using the form. The *Report* also refers to common usage that 'embraces the singular "they" form more often than the supposedly "grammatically correct" everyone/everybody/he/ him/his form', and concludes, in relation to legislation:

> Where legislation is drafted in gender specific terms, the Committee can see no reason for continuing the practice. It is unnecessary, is the subject of controversy amongst significant sectors of the community, and is not readily understood by laypeople.
> (Parliament of Victoria, Legal and Constitutional Committee 1983, p. 146)

If sixteenth- and seventeenth-century English grammarians tried ignorantly and unnecessarily to proscribe usage that seemed to them to be illogical (apparently not knowing, or not caring, about polite plural address forms in other languages, e.g. *vous* in French), then twentieth-century linguists, with hopefully a little more understanding of the complex interrelationship of language and culture, can support a return to *they*, the traditional colloquial choice of speakers of English. Kramer et al. (1978) suggest that

> the situation of the singular 'they' may be one of progress toward acceptance. Its persistence over the centuries suggests, first, that the speech community does feel the strain of referring to females with the masculine, and, second, that this is the weak point of sexist language, the point at which it may break.
>
> (Kramer et al., 1978, p. 650)

Lexical resources: *man* and *woman*

The vocabulary, or lexis, of a language is the most obvious repository of the meanings of *man* and *woman* in English-speaking societies. As we shall see in the next section, there are less obvious ways in which lexical meanings are reinforced, in the grammar of the language.

What lexis does is to name activities or processes, people and things associated with those activities or processes, and characteristics or attributes of those activities or processes, people, and things, in ways that are culturally salient. To undertake a complete analysis of the lexical resources of English with respect to gender would be immensely revealing but a mammoth task that has not yet been attempted. What will be done here is simply to indicate some of the issues and the general direction that the findings of a larger analysis seem likely to take.

See Schulz (1975) and Stanley (1977) for extremely interesting forays into the analysis of lexical resources of English with respect to gender.

There are two kinds of authoritative record of the lexical resources of English, the thesaurus and the dictionary. A thesaurus provides the more comprehensive listing of words related to one another in terms of meaning. It is organised taxonomically (though the nature of those taxonomic relations is implicit rather than explicit). A dictionary provides an explicit account of the meanings of individual words and is organised purely alphabetically. Dictionary meanings are primarily referential: where evaluative meaning is involved this will usually be handled by using terms such as 'used pejoratively' or 'with a diminutive flavour'. An examination of dictionary entries for *man* and *woman* can readily include derived forms (*womanise, manliness*), compound forms (*womanfolk, manpower*), and fixed structural collocations (*women's rights, man in the street*). But little indication can be given, with this kind of lexical organisation, of the larger set of items that these are related to. What does show up very clearly is a considerable difference in the numbers of terms based on *man* and *woman*. In both the *Shorter Oxford English Dictionary* and the *Macquarie Dictionary* the ratio of *man* words to *woman* words is nearly 3:1.

The sequential presentation of the entries *male* and *female* (at 372 and 373 respectively) in *Roget's Thesaurus* (1962 and 1982 editions) somewhat reverses this imbalance, with the entry for *female* being one and a half times the length of that for *male* (in both editions). There would seem to be several reasons for this discrepancy. Firstly, a thesaurus can appropriately include a selection of the proliferation of pejorative lexis referring to women (Schulz (1975, p.72), 'located roughly a thousand words and phrases describing women in sexually derogatory ways'). A dictionary cannot include this kind of lexis under *woman* unless the forms of the words make this appropriate. Thus items like *kept woman* and *scarlet woman* are included in the *Macquarie Dictionary*, but not the set of items *moll, bint, crumpet, bit of fluff, broad, courtesan*, cross-referenced to 952 *loose woman*, which lists in total eighty-six words for women as sexually active/available (excluding proper names) (*Roget's Thesaurus* 1982). At least four other words found under 952 referring to women also appear under 373 *female*, making a total of well over 10 per cent of the total set. The comparable set of terms referring to males as sexually active is smaller (55 items listed at 952, excluding terms referring to homosexual men—whose location under the general heading *libertine* is ideologically revealing—and men two-timed or cuckolded). But only just over 5 per cent is found listed at 372 *male*. In other words, the already existing discrepancy in the language is being compounded by the compilers of the thesaurus—in ways that are ideologically perfectly comprehensible, of course. (The question of different evaluative weightings on the female and male terms involving sexual activity will be raised below.)

A second reason why the thesaurus entry is longer for *female* than for *male*, while dictionaries reverse this weighting, is that while dictionaries can appropriately include items that derive from the word *man* even when the meaning is not specifically and exclusively male (e.g. *manhole, man-made, manslaughter*) this cannot be done in a thesaurus. It may well be the case that the dictionary itself, with its emphasis on similarity of form because of its alphabetical organisation, and being a far more familiar lexical resource than the thesaurus, has played some role in such items being seen as implicitly male. Such implicit gender, however, cannot be readily handled in a thesaurus and certainly not in a dictionary, as dictionaries are currently conceived and organised. It is best handled grammatically.

A complete taxonomic account of all lexis relating to *man/woman* would also ideally take into account the multitude of terms referring to people involved in various activities/processes, where the existence of forms marked with a feminine suffix (principally *-ess*) or modified in some way to indicate a female referent (e.g. *woman doctor, girl reporter*) implicitly defines all terms not so marked as male. That is to say, the (linguistically) unmarked term, the linguistic (and cultural) norm, is the male, and suffixed and modified forms of this 'norm' represent a departure, a deviation. Experimental evidence, referred to above with reference to generic *he*, clearly indicates that supposedly generic *man* and compounds including it (*chairman, alderman*) are perceived as male, not as unmarked with respect to gender. Given the findings reported by Graham (1975) that over seven times as many men as women appeared in books read by school children and over twice as many boys as girls, such an interpretation is hardly surprising. Males are simply more visible, creating the presumption that if someone is doing something it's likely to be a male unless actually specified as a female.

Three important issues concerning the structure of the lexicon concerning woman and man emerge from investigating available codified resources. The first is the question of asymmetry between male and female, or looked at from another point of view, of gaps in the lexicon. Such asymmetry, leading to gaps, arises in the first instance from the

This issue will be taken up in more detail in Chapter 4 in discussing gender as a covert grammatical category.

cultural circumstances of women's and men's permitted and actual spheres of activity. It subsequently becomes a way of enforcing the perpetuation of such differentiated spheres of activity. As long as such gaps are simply not perceived, women will not see themselves as excluded from 'men's' areas nor vice versa, and hence will not be in a position to aspire to other roles and activities than those conventionally available to them. And even after some awareness of such lexical gaps develops, their existence can be used as a justification for explicitly and consciously excluding people from spheres other than the traditional ones, on the grounds that to go outside these legitimated spheres is impossible/ immoral/ improper/ unnatural/wrong. Ideology now begins to be visible, buttressing and justifying existing social practice.

A simple listing of the areas of female and male experience that do not have comparable sets of entries for the other gender in the 1982 edition of *Roget's Thesaurus* makes some of the gaps clear. This edition does fill some of the gaps in the 1962 edition by including lexis that is either new or that was excluded from the 1962 edition. Note that objects such as *Roget's Thesaurus*, the *Oxford English Dictionary*, and the *Macquarie Dictionary* must be treated as cultural artifacts, themselves influenced by ideology. Thus, the 1982 edition of *Roget's Thesaurus* includes lexis that indicates that what looked like gaps in the language in the earlier edition were not really so, but were an ideologically influenced artifact of that earlier period—prior to the 1960s-70s women's movement. The 1982 edition accurately indicates the existence of many real gaps, but some of its inexplicable omissions of regularly occurring items imply gaps that do not actually exist. Thus are stereotypes perpetuated.

The salient categories subsuming words for *woman* (consisting of a single lexical item in some cases; in others, many items) are shown in Table 3.3. The salient categories subsuming words for *man* that can be identified but have no parallel in the lexis for *woman* are given in Table 3.4.

These lists, particularly when one takes into account the attitude, or ideologically derived evaluation, attached to the category as a whole, give a fairly clear account of how woman and man are thought of by speakers of English. This can be summed up by saying that women are valued positively when they are young, beloved, married, and the producer/nurturer of children, but negatively when they are sexual, unmarried, verbally aggressive, demanding rights, or aspiring to govern themselves or others. Men are valued negatively when they are either excessively 'masculine', or macho (mostly by women but by some men also), or insufficiently masculine, i.e. effeminate, (stereotypically) homosexual. Otherwise they are mostly valued positively.

Finally, two issues need to be raised. The first is why lexis proliferates in certain categories, to what sometimes seems an absurd and unnecessary degree, and seems to keep on doing so. The prime instances are woman-as-prostitute, where *Roget's Thesaurus* (1982) lists 88 items and Stanley (1977) identified 220, and man-as-everyday-basic-human, where the number of items involved is not nearly as great, but

Table 3.3   Salient categories subsuming words for *woman*

'womanness'	(Latinate words indicating this is viewed as a technical matter—maybe a problem of the nineteenth-century debate on 'the woman question')
women's rights	
women's medical issues	
women's quarters	
virginity	
unmarried state	(undesirability thereof)
working women	('marked', i.e. unnatural: indicated by using compounds with either a male word (*bachelor girl*) or a word referring to women's 'real' role (*working mother*))
young womanhood	(positively valued when ethereal and untouchable, negatively when sexually available)
hair colour	(positive insofar as indicating sexual attract-iveness, negative as indicating sexuality and nothing else)
prostitute/ loose woman	(strongly negative—compare different evaluation of males as sexually active)
verbal aggression	(extremely negative, hostile)
woman as goddess	(valued as beautiful and untouchable, i.e. the antithesis of woman as prostitute)
motherhood	(bearer and nurturer of children: strongly valued)
mature wifehood	
widowed woman of standing	(i.e. *dowager*)
government of women	(at best viewed uneasily (*matriarchy*); at worst, very negatively, as in *regiment of women* — presumably the monstrous one of John Knox)

Note: Evaluative loadings indicated by parenthetical comments.

Table 3.4   Salient categories subsuming words for *man* that have no parallel for *woman*

mateship	
machismo	(positive or negative depending on the point of view: from that of women's rights (*male chauvinist*) it is clearly negative)
everyday humanness	(a large number of positively valued, but in a low-key way, items such as *guy*, *bloke*, *chap*)
male as escort	(of female)
'gay dog'	(the cross-reference is to 952 *libertine*, which is more negatively valued than any of the terms included under 372 *man*—or under *libertine*)
family man	(not negative—but contrast with other male categories)

where the items themselves seem absolutely synonymous. Stanley suggests one explanation for the proliferation of woman-as-prostitute words in the following terms:

> The very size of the set and the impossibility of collecting **all** the terms for prostitute is a comment on our culture. As linguists, we assume that the existence of a new lexical item indicates a cultural need for a term that expresses a new concept. Isn't it strange that the set of terms that refer to prostitutes is one that's constantly expanding? If there is a cultural need, surely it is that only of men, defining and asserting their 'masculinity' through their use of women's bodies.
>
> (Stanley, 1977, p. 310)

In linguistic terms, such proliferation is characteristic of slang (Wescott, 1976/1980, p.80) and antilanguages (Halliday, 1976) and occurs in intimate relationships with respect to terms of address (Poynton, 1984). Its driving force would appear to be the primacy of interpersonal meaning in the context of special relationships, whether special by virtue of sexual intimacy or solidary bonding inside or outside mainstream social groupings (peer groups or outsider groups like jail populations or criminals). While experiential meaning—meaning concerning events and the participants and circumstances involved in them—is economical in terms of lexis (one word to one meaning) and characteristically employs constituency-type structures in grammar, interpersonal meaning characteristically employs very different kinds of structures, which are strung out repetitively throughout a clause. Lexical proliferation would seem to be this prosodic mode of functioning operating at the level of lexis.

Stanley is right then in seeing men as the source of the lexical proliferation she deals with: the solidarity of males, the mateship of men, provides the interpersonal context for the proliferation of lexis about both women and men, as men interpret them ideologically.

Presumably something of the same set of factors can be invoked to explain a further lexical phenomenon: the persistent historical tendency for words referring to women to become pejorative in meaning and to do so in a very specific way, by acquiring sexual overtones. Words like *mistress*, *hussy*, *broad*, and *spinster* did not originally have the pejorative and/or sexual meanings they have today. Given the legal, moral, and even physical constraints on women's freedom to realise their sexuality that have been found in English-speaking societies for many centuries, it would seem that it is not women's behaviour but rather men's fears—and fantasies—about women's sexuality, and their refusal to take women seriously as other than sexual beings, that has motivated such a consistent pattern of derogation. This pattern would seem to be a particularly blatant instance of ideology in action, skewing the lexical resources of the language by 'naming' women in ways that have contributed to the perpetuation of distorted images of them (particularly by men) and, even more significantly, to the negative self-image of women themselves.

See Schulz (1975) for an account of this phenomenon, called there 'semantic derogation'.

Chapter 4

Speaking about men and women

Introduction

Social life, in terms of institutions and roles, is socially constructed. The potentially almost limitless range of possibilities for human behaviour is, in practice, constrained for most individuals, who see the flouter of social constraints as behaving un-naturally, and not themselves. They do not perceive these constraints on their behaviour as constraints. The particular facts of this social construction are, to a considerable extent, named (lexicalised) and those 'facts', as 'meanings', become part of the language used by members of that society. This naming takes place not in isolation from, but in the context of, a socially constructed understanding of the relations between 'things' (including people, objects, and ideas) and 'events' (including doing, perceiving, saying, and even being), which also becomes part of the language: its grammar, looked at from the perspective of experiential meaning, language as representation.

It is important to understand that lexis without structure is not language. The common equation of lexis with language is probably, in part at least, an artifact of literate cultures possessing such objects as dictionaries and thesauruses. Though much harder to grasp, the notion of structure without lexis is, in fact, more meaningful: the structures of language can be seen as resources for relating 'things' and 'events' in culturally meaningful ways—which may mean (and commonly does) that such relations are conceived of in terms of an older world-view that may not accord very well with a changing social reality.

The experiential structures that will be the focus of this chapter occur in language with two degrees of specificity:

1. relations between 'things' and 'events' may be spelled out in relation to one another in CLAUSE STRUCTURE, e.g.

   Alice works sixteen hours a day
   David owns a Burmese cat

2. relations between 'things' and 'events' may be handled in a more associational way, realised as attributes of someone or something, in NOMINAL GROUP STRUCTURE, e.g.

   workaholic Alice
   David's Burmese cat

Field

Neither structure normally occurs by itself (outside of books about language!): just as nominal groups are generally part of clauses, clauses themselves are part of ongoing discourse. Such discourse may be spoken or written, produced individually or constructed co-operatively by two or more people. In the construction of texts, structures, and more particularly the lexis used in them (since structures are more general than lexis), cluster in characteristic configurations that signal that speakers are acting within or reflecting upon certain FIELDS—portions of socially constructed experience recognised as discrete portions by members of that culture, commonly institutionalised to the extent of having a name (e.g. athletics, music) or maybe even to the extent of being identifiable as a formally constituted social institution (e.g. government, education).

See Halliday & Hasan (1989); and Plum (1984).

The socially constructed world functions by distributing access to roles and activities in relation to what are regarded as relevant social characteristics such as age, gender, class, etc. Some roles and activities, of course, do distribute themselves: men cannot give birth to a child, nor young children cope with many adult tasks—though children in Third World countries are by no means the helpless, irresponsible tots of the Western World. It is probably more accurate to speak of restricted, rather than simply distributed, access to roles and activities. Where such restriction of access to fields exists with respect to any social characteristic, then one can expect this to show up linguistically in terms of differences in what people talk about and in differences in how people are talked about.

There is considerable evidence that the fields of discourse tend to differ for men and women and that, as a consequence of this, topics of conversation (one manifestation of field) differ, as well as grammatical structures (the means by which field and topic, and women and men themselves, are talked about). Many fields are identifiable as male or female on the basis of both acknowledged and unacknowledged restricted access (discrimination) and on the basis of what people say. Quotations included in *The National Times—Women's Role* (1983) indicate that many men see the fields of sport, local government, the stock market, economics, wine, and hospital administration (among others) as being male and many women concur. Tamara Fraser, married to former Prime Minister Malcolm Fraser, replied when asked 'a complicated economic question':

> Oh, come on, you're talking to a girl now.
> *(National Times—Women's Role* 1983, p. 103)

And observations of mainly women staff in one department of an American telephone company indicated that they avoided the fields of politics and religion, unlike men in other departments, because they saw these as 'properly in the domain of men' (Langer, 1970, reported in Eakins & Eakins, 1978, p.74)

The prime women's fields, as seen by both women and men, are domestic and personal (e.g. reproduction, human relationships, child-rearing, domestic work—including shopping, cooking, washing, housecleaning, cosmetics, fashion, and home decoration). It is worth noting that, directly relatable to the question of the status of these fields in our society, which is not high, is the fact that on the whole they do not have an elaborated technical lexis, control of which is a necessary prerequisite to claims to expert status in this society. Where such lexis has been elaborated, for instance in child psychology (where it is decidedly a moot point whether any greater insight into the rearing of children has been gained than has been in the possession of generations of women charged with the job as mothers, grandmothers, aunts, etc.), or in French cuisine, it is commonly the case that it is men rather than women who learn the language and become the acknowledged experts.

The most obvious manifestation of field is TOPIC and there is plenty of evidence that women and men do talk about different topics. In Betsy Wearing's study of Australian mothers, working-class women talked to one another about 'children and the problems associated with babies and children, general topics, the house and household things, husbands and other people, family life and television' (Wearing, 1984, pp.170-1); middle-class women talked about 'children and child related problems . . . entertainments, sports, travel, holidays' (p.177); and women who belong to consciousness-raising groups talked about 'relationships with husband, the division of labour in the home, relationship, [sic] with their own mother, relationships with children and labour both inside and outside the home' (p.181).

Several American studies of conversation overheard in public places are summarised by Eakins and Eakins, who conclude:

> Men's greatest conversational interests seemed to be business and money, followed by sports and amusements. Women's leading topics were men and clothes. Persons played a smaller part in men's talk and a larger part in women's.
>
> (Eakins & Eakins, 1978, p. 74)

(Eakins and Eakins had previously referred to figures from one study which found that 37 per cent of women's conversation, but only 16 per cent of men's, was concerned with 'persons' as a topic.)

Grammatical structure: the nominal group

The second way in which field is both manifested itself and has further implications with respect to gender is in terms of grammatical struc-tures. Men and women are talked about differently, not only in terms of the characteristic roles, activities, and objects that are associated with them on the basis of the fields that they are known to be involved in and that are perceived as appropriate for them to engage in (differences that will come out as lexical differences, words characteristically associated with, or seen as, female and male), but also in terms of differ-ences in the perceived centrality or marginality of their participation in the affairs of the world (differences that will come out as grammat-ical differences, particularly involving participant roles in clause structure).

To deal first with the question of lexical choice in relation to gender, it has often been pointed out that women are frequently primarily characterised in terms of their appearance, their marital status, and their fecundity (the 'happily married for thirty years, still attractive mother of five' style of newspaper description, used both for women coming to public attention because of some achievement/action of their own and for women who happen to be married to, or the parent of, someone else in the news). The basis of frequently voiced objections to such characterisation is that it is irrelevant, and hence offensive, and that it perpetuates a stereotyped view of women (the youth, beauty, and motherhood syndrome). What is proposed instead is that women and men should be characterised in parallel terms, that only in contexts where it is appropriate for a man's personal appearance or domestic arrangements to be referred to should it be appropriate to refer to a woman's. Nice examples of the sort of practice objected to are the following, again from *The National Times—Women's Role:*

> Dr Rosendale, a slender brunette who specialises in short-term economic predictions
>
> (p. 34)
>
> This rather sweet young woman is actually a real estate giant.
>
> (p. 31)

The problem is that to simply delete the feminine markers (stereotypic or not) would effectively identify these individuals as male, not simply because more economists and real-estate personnel are male than female but because gender is built into the heart of the English classification of the 'things' of the world in terms of its nouns.

Evidence indicating that non-animate nouns, and animate but non-human nouns, are marked for gender to an extent not formally recognised has already been referred to with respect to pronoun choice and the phenomenon known as personification in both everyday informal conversation and children's stories. Our focus now will be on animate human nouns, those used to refer to people. Many of these, particularly occupational and professional labels, are commonly said to be unmarked for gender or of common gender. In fact they are covertly male: the pervasive habit of indicating by some linguistic marker when a woman is being referred to is so pervasive that the absence of such an indicator is taken to mean that the referent is a man. Thus the male is linguistically unmarked, the linguistic norm, and the female has to be seen as a deviation from that norm. The three techniques used to mark feminine gender/femaleness of referent are: the addition of a suffix to the noun, using a word explicitly marking the referent as female (*woman, girl,* etc.), and using a word implicitly marking the referent as female (*pretty, brunette, emotional,* etc.).

The most common feminine suffix is *-ess*. Words in current use include *actress, hostess, deaconess, stewardess, manageress, waitress, mayoress, mistress, goddess, princess*. Others either going out of use or never widely used include *adventuress, authoress, cateress, negress, inventress, professoress, murderess, sculptress, oratress*. Yet others have been proposed, facetiously and seriously, including *teacheress, singeress, barristress,* even *secretaress*. The third edition of the *Shorter Oxford English Dictionary* (1973) noted under *-ess* that

58

. . . the agent-nouns in *-er*, and the sbs. [i.e. substantives] indicating profession etc., are now treated as of common gender, whenever possible.

It is not entirely clear whether the *Shorter Oxford English Dictionary* is referring to its own practice or to general practice, but it does seem to have been the case that the use of such forms has been declining in the twentieth century and that attitudes have changed considerably. One indication of this change is that while the first edition in 1926 of Fowler's *Modern English Usage* advocated the use and coinage of such marked forms on the grounds that 'everyone knows the inconvenience of being uncertain whether a doctor is a man or woman' (cited in Miller & Swift, 1977, p. 43), the second edition, revised by Sir Ernest Gowers in 1965, noted that 'feminine designations seem now to be falling into disuse' and suggested that the explanation for this might be that it

> symbolizes the victory of women in their struggle for equal rights; it reflects the abandonment by men of those ideas about women in the professions that moved Dr Johnson to his rude remark about women preachers. Modern woman justifiably resents any such implications.
>
> (Fowler, 1965, pp. 194-5)

That the battle is by no means won is indicated, however, by the fact that some of these suffixed forms, which had been disappearing, re-surfaced in the 1970s 'suggesting a backlash (conscious or otherwise) to the women's movement' (Miller & Swift, 1981, p.100). Miller and Swift note Gloria Steinem, founder and editor of *Ms* magazine, referred to as an *editress* and Sylvia Plath as *poetess*, as well as some of those opposed to women's ordination within the Christian churches referring to *priestesses*—the pejorative intention here being very evident.

The other suffix much less commonly used, generally pejoratively and/or facetiously, is *-ette*. Among the few instances of forms using this suffix to pass into general usage are *usherette* and *suffragette*—the latter particularly ironic, since the women who fought for the suffrage in the late nineteenth and early twentieth centuries referred to themselves as *suffragists* and the word *suffragette* was first using in 1906 by the *Daily Mail* in a deliberate attempt to trivialise these women and their aims (Miller & Swift, 1981, p.107). Other *-ette* forms that have been coined are more revealing of what was likely to have been the original force of that put-down of the suffragists, akin in its force to today's reference to feminists as *women's libbers*: *conductorette, announcerette, undergraduette, farmerette, astronette, martyrette* (re suffragist women), *bachelorette*, and *Redskinette*. As Miller and Swift (1981, p.100) remark with reference to several of these, including the last, forms like this 'effectively define females as part of a sideshow'.

The second technique for indicating that a human referent is female is by using a word explicitly indicating this (e.g. *woman, lady, female, girl*) in combination with the occupational or agent word, producing such forms as *woman doctor, lady lawyer, female attendant*, and *girl reporter*. Female words used in this way, as classifiers, perform a particular kind of modification of the head word of the nominal group indicating a sub-class of the group referred to. Identifying a sub-class of a group as female of course carries the implication that the group itself is basically male.

> In systemic-functional grammar they are **classifiers** (Halliday 1985).

59

Not only are head words and classifiers in nominal groups frequently marked for gender, so is another type of functional element modifying the head: the epithet (modifying the head in terms of what like rather than what kind, as classifiers do). Where classifiers are commonly nouns, and hence can be explicitly gender words or gender-marked, epithets are characteristically adjectives. As Kress and Hodge (1979) show, and as emerges from adjective check lists in psychological studies referring to female and male, adjectives themselves are by no means as neutral in terms of gender as one might be inclined to think.

The following tables list adjectives associated with women and men, together with an evaluative classification of each adjective, in a study by Williams and Bennett (1975) as reported in Archer and Lloyd (1982, pp. 38-39). The tables list those adjectives (out of an original list of 300) that were agreed upon as male or female by 75 per cent of the total number of subjects, 30 describing women and 33 describing men. The evaluative classification is positive, negative, or neutral, indicated by +, −, and 0.

Table 4.1 Adjectives associated with women, with evaluative classification

Affected	−	Feminine	0	Prudish	−
Affectionate	+	Fickle	−	Rattle-brained	−
Appreciative	+	Flirtatious	0	Sensitive	0
Attractive	+	Frivolous	−	Sentimental	0
Charming	+	Fussy	−	Soft-hearted	0
Complaining	−	Gentle	+	Sophisticated	0
Dependent	0	High-strung	0	Submissive	0
Dreamy	0	Meek	0	Talkative	0
Emotional	0	Mild	0	Weak	−
Excitable	0	Nagging	−	Whiny	−

Source: Archer & Lloyd (1983), p. 38, adapted from Williams & Bennett (1975)

Table 4.2 Adjectives associated with men, with evaluative classification

Adventurous	+	Disorderly	−	Realistic	+
Aggressive	0	Dominant	0	Robust	0
Ambitious	+	Enterprising	+	Self-confident	0
Assertive	0	Forceful	0	Severe	0
Autocratic	0	Handsome	0	Stable	+
Boastful	−	Independent	+	Steady	0
Coarse	−	Jolly	0	Stern	0
Confident	+	Logical	+	Strong	0
Courageous	+	Loud	−	Tough	0
Cruel	0	Masculine	0	Unemotional	0
Daring	−	Rational	+	Unexcitable	0

Source: Archer & Lloyd (1983), p. 39, adapted from Williams & Bennett (1975)

It should, of course, be pointed out that the tasks that produce such findings have little or nothing to do with the questions of COLLOCATION, the tendency of words to habitually appear together in structures (e.g. *pretty girl*, *stern father*) and, in a more dispersed fashion, throughout texts. Work on lexical relations in general (including collocation) with gender in mind would presumably be revealing, but it would need to be done on a very large scale.

Nominal groups referring to persons, then, are hardly neutral with respect to gender. If the referent is female then that fact is likely to be indicated using one or more of the linguistic resources available, and if femaleness is not marked then the assumption will be that the referent is male. And this assumption can show up with the most innocuous and least apparently gender-marked items—such as in the cable report of a news event that referred to 'two people and a stewardess' who were killed in an explosion on a ship and the twelve-year-old boy who told his mother that there were 'six kids in my French class and fifteen girls' (*National Times—Women's Role* 1983, pp.14, 17). Or the innocuous little news report that began:

A young East German crossed the Berlin Wall last night under a hail of bullets from East German border guards, police said today. The German, aged 22, used a ladder to scale the wall and cross over into the French sector of West Berlin.

The next clause begins with a pronoun referring to the border-crosser and it will hardly come as a surprise to learn that that pronoun is *he*: characterisation in terms of occupation, nationality, abilities—in fact anything other than youth, beauty, and motherhood—generally implies that the referent is male unless one is told to the contrary. If the border-crosser had been female, this information would undoubtedly have been given at the very beginning of the news report: we would have been told whether she was attractive, romantically attached, probably what colour her hair and/or eyes were—and her age could certainly not have been left until the second sentence.

The question that now must be asked about gender marking is: why? Why does it matter that female referents must be identified as such? And what is the effect of the various kinds of marking? The basic issue seems to concern power. Eakins and Eakins put it very nicely when they note, after having referred to the weakening, diminishing, or trivialising effect of feminine suffixes such as *-ess* or *-ette*, that:

the male terms carry the suggestion of added power or competency. Or, put in another way, **adding** a feminine marker ending may **detract** from connotations of potency that such a word normally evokes in people.
(Eakins & Eakins, 1978, p.115)

In other words being powerful matters, but women are not supposed to be powerful, so by marking the references to them as female, even when the roles they play in the society are in fact powerful and prestigious, that power and prestige are diminished and discounted.

There is yet another issue to be raised concerning modification in nominal groups in relation to such paired examples as the following (from a film review):

The unemployed 19-year-old Cal
(who falls in love with)
a pretty Catholic librarian

Apart from the fact that the referents are clearly male and female, respectively, there is a curious effect in the second group whereby the very presence of the word *pretty* leaches out some of the experiential force of *Catholic* (important in that the film in which these two are characters is set in contemporary Northern Ireland) and *librarian* (a job for which a relatively high level of education is required and which consequently has a certain amount of prestige attached to it). It is hard to take seriously a *Catholic librarian* who is *pretty*—a *19-year-old Catholic librarian* would be someone a little more substantial. Age is a significant diminisher of potency but gender is more powerful, it would seem.

The linguistic status of *pretty* in the example cited would seem to be the key to understanding what is going on: it is attitudinal as well as referential but probably more strongly the former, i.e. it is interpersonal. Interpersonal meanings habitually spread themselves through linguistic structures, and what seems to be happening here is that the interpersonal force of the word, bolstered by ideological considerations, is spreading into the more experientially oriented part of the group. Further, the word *pretty* itself invokes those genres where all that is required of a woman is that she be young and attractive (and unattached), everything else being irrelevant background information, but where a man is expected to be someone of substance, both personally and in the public world of affairs. Women are always liable to be represented as if they're characters from a Mills and Boon romance, but one does have a choice with men—even within the pages of the romance. A man can be characterised as

> the professional civil servant from an orthodox department, a man to handle paper and integrate the brilliance of his staff with the cumbersome machine of bureaucracy.
>
> (Le Carré, 1964, p.13)

Or he can be characterised as the hero of this Mills & Boon romance:

> a man with grey eyes and a commanding mouth, with dark hair and a midnight-blue voice, whose arms were strong and secure.
>
> (Ker, 1984, pp.14-15)

In either case, of course, he is a figure to reckon with, a figure of substance and power.

Grammatical structure: the clause

The same issue of power and powerlessness emerges clearly at clause rank in relation principally to the question of agency: whether or not one is presented as doing or being done to, as causer of actions/events or merely acted upon, what one is presented as acting upon, whether events are presented as occurring with or without agency. The most obvious issues to investigate are:

• the frequency of women compared to men in the role of agent;
• the nature of the processes involved;
• the nature of what is at the receiving end of the doing of agents; and
• what kinds of agents involved in what kinds of processes get deleted.

Not a great deal of work has been done with clause structure, but what there is suggests the answers below.

On agent deletion (achieved by using passive rather than active forms and taking up the option that this structure makes available of deleting the agent): women as agents, especially in creative activity, may tend to be deleted. Mainardi (1973) noted, in her research into quilting as 'women's unrecognised art',

> the constant use of the passive voice in reference to quilts ('quilts were made', 'quilting was done', 'names changed', never 'women made quilts', 'women changed the names').
> (Mainardi, 1973, p.68, cited in Thorne & Henley, 1975b, pp. 218-19)

Men as agents may also be deleted, when what they might otherwise be held responsible for is politically sensitive or ideologically uncomfortable (remembering that *wars are waged* rather than *men wage wars*). Salem (1980), in an analysis of Virginia Woolf's *A Room of One's Own*, suggests that through her use of the 'truncated passive' (i.e. agent deleted),

> Woolf actually obscures the agentive role men have played in the oppression of women, often shifting the focus onto women as culpable for their own plight, and defusing the force of her observations.
> (Salem, 1980, p.210)

Thus Woolf's grammar is at odds with what her overall argument has been taken to be.

Shuster (1973, 1974, abstracted in Thorne & Henley, 1975b, p. 236 and summarised in Eakins & Eakins, 1978, pp. 120-1) suggests that passive forms are more common if females are speaking or being referred to, with respect to certain verbs involving sexual or courting activity, e.g. *to be laid, to be fucked, to be taken* (sexually), *to be walked* (home), *to be picked up*. The (female) passive examples cited in Eakins and Eakins all have the male agent present but they sound marked. Compare

She was picked up in a bar

and

She was picked up by him in a bar.

The less marked pattern would seem to be to delete the agent when the female is subject. In the active form the male is of necessity Subject and Actor. Shuster suggests the active form is more characteristically used by and about males. It may be the case that Woolf is exemplifying a more general female pattern, reflecting the female internalisation of culturally-expected 'passivity'—and an understandable hesitancy about naming men as oppressors, given the power they do wield.

On the likelihood of women and men appearing as agents: Thwaite (1983) investigated three Mills and Boon romances in a deliberate attempt to identify ideologically motivated structures. Her data thus possibly exaggerates tendencies in the language used about men and women in less ideologically loaded genres but cannot be seen as inventing patterns totally arbitrarily or randomly. Thwaite found that in clauses with material (doing) processes, the female participant had things done to her more often than the male, who was more often the Doer (Thwaite, 1983, p.145) and that where a process was coded as having a Causer, the male was far more likely than the female to fill this role (p.151). Thwaite found that differences between the sexes showed up most clearly with respect to material processes and suggests a likely reason is that

> if one wishes to exert power, it is more effective to exert it within the domain of 'doing' rather than, for example 'sensing', 'saying' or 'behaving'. It may also be more difficult to control these other types of process: . . . it is not easy to influence how people **think**, compared with using physical force to influence how they **act**.
>
> (Thwaite, 1983, p.152)

On what an agent has control over: Hellinger (1980) found that women as agents in clauses involving 'personal achievement, creative action, or some prestigious professional activity' were almost non-existent in English language text-books used in German schools: three instances were identified—1.3 per cent of the total instances of clauses with female agents. The largest category involved action directed at a male (including *she shook him by the shoulder; feed their husbands instant coffee*) and the next largest involved verbs of speaking (where the relevant participant role is that of Sayer rather than Actor in systemic-functional terms). Hellinger sees this as supporting 'the popular stereotype that speaking is one of the most essential female activities' (1980, p. 272)—noting that, in the text books examined, men spoke four times as often as women—and suggests that 'speaking often functions as substitute for other types of behaviour in women' (1980, p. 273).

By far the most detailed investigation of what women have control over when they function as agents is that carried out by Thwaite (1983). She found that women controlled clothing and accessories, their own body parts, and 'many small parts of the domestic environment' (Thwaite, 1983, p. 160) but never anything as important as a lease, cash, or a car, all controlled by males. Again, the extent of the restriction of female control is undoubtedly exaggerated in this data in relation to the actual extent of women's control in the 'real world' (which certainly includes, for many, lease, cash, and car), but the discrepancy in range and significance of what is in the control of females and what in the control of males in these romances seems only an exaggerated version of the discrepancy between the legitimated extent of men's and women's power that was dealt with earlier in this chapter.

The extent of that power has, of course, changed so that there may be three versions of the extent of women's real control: the version portrayed in romances and other genres functioning as fairly direct realisations of ideology, the version portrayed in other somewhat less ideologically constructed discourse, and the version that 'is' in the 'real world' out there. As what actually happens gets more out of step with ideology, many people begin to perceive the discrepancies—and to protest and demand change. Others, however, look right through language as if it were a pane of clear glass, failing to realise that it is somewhat more like a lens or even a mirror, beaming back to the constructed social world its own inventions, thereby ensuring that for the most part the mirror itself, language, is simply invisible—and hence invisible too the role it plays in ensuring the perpetuation of a constructed reality. The fact that we can turn language back on itself—use it to look at itself—offers us a possible way out of what otherwise would be a permanent situation of the relationship of language to 'reality' being one of self-fulfilling prophecy.

Chapter 5

Speaking as woman/man

Stereotypes and interpretations

It is not difficult to identify figures in folklore and popular culture that embody stereotypes of male and female as speaker. There is The Mouth, who produces an unending stream of vacuous inanities, never letting anyone else get a word in if it can be prevented and never listening to them (or themself, for that matter) if they do manage to make a breach in the wall of words. The Mouth may be adult or adolescent; the immature version is The Chatterbox. There is The Knowall (sometimes also called The Professor), who can be any age from eight upwards and who knows everything there is to know about one particular topic (e.g. cricket, lizards, the Labour Party, jazz, etc.) and insists on telling you all about it whether you want to know or not, turning every conversation to their pet topic. Terminal Knowall cases know everything about everything—including your own field of expertise (which they have never studied) but it stands to reason, doesn't it . . .?

Then there is The Life of the Party, with a never-ending store of jokes and anecdotes, some of which may be a bit, well, EXPLICIT, but all in fun, all in fun. And as the night wears on and the grog runs through, the jokes get MORE explicit . . . and the party can't wind up (or down) until The Life of the Party goes home. There's also Daddy's Little Girl who always appears attached, limpet-like, to some male at whom she directs coaxings, cooings, and blandishments with a strict eye to profit: fur coats and Porsches, dishwashers, more pocket money, fully accoutremented Barbie and Ken dolls of her very own. Her cousin is Daddy's Sweet Loving Little Girl, who also coaxes, coos, and blandishes but for Daddy's good, not her own. In some quarters she is regarded as a half-wit, in others, as the model of self-sacrificing womanhood.

There is The Perfect Lady, whose vowels are pure, whose grammar is impeccable, who would never let a profanity escape her lips or a euphemism remain unuttered, and who always knows the right thing to say on social occasions. (She knows all about etiquette.) The Perfect Lady comes in a Basilisk version, who would not blush at The Life of the Party, and a Super-Refined version, who would. There is The Strong

Silent Type who believes that words are for making people jump to it and that any other use of them is superfluous.

There is a range of further characters, including The Con Artist (who'll talk his way into your bed or you out of your money), The Ballbreaker (several versions including The Educated Woman, The Classic Nag, and, most terrifying of all, The Man-Hating Feminist Lesbian, who won't even talk to men), The Harassed Housewife (who pitches all conversation at the two-year-old level), and others. All of these characters are recognisable, and recognisable as female or male, even when no overt signal of gender was given in the label. This leads to three points that need to be made.

Firstly, there is no single stereotype of how women and men talk in this society, but there are a number of stereotypic portraits on the basis of which a few generalisations have been made: women speak 'better' (more 'correctly' and with more 'refined' accents) than men; men swear and use slang more than women; women and men talk about different things; men tell jokes and women can't; women can smooth over difficult social situations; and men find this more difficult. And both women and men, in appropriate settings, are capable of talking people to death, though it is the female who has the more pervasive reputation as a talker, an entirely unjustified one in terms of male-female interaction (where all available evidence indicates that males talk more than females), whose origin must be presumed to be ideological. Dale Spender sees the origin of the 'chattering female' stereotype in the following terms:

> Behind the constantly reiterated assertion that females are the talkative sex an implicit comparison is being made against some standard or norm. It has been generally accepted that females talk more than males but it is only necessary to tape a conversation at a social gathering, a trade union meeting or in a classroom to find that it is males who do the talking. The yardstick against which women's talk is, in fact, measured is that of **silence**. 'Silence gives the proper grace to women', wrote Sophocles in *Ajax* and his sentiments are still echoed in today's image of the desirable woman. When silence is considered the appropriate behaviour for women then, quite conveniently in a sexist society, almost any talk a woman engages in can be considered too much!
>
> (Spender, 1980a, p. 148)

Some of these characteristics of the stereotypic female/male speaker, those involving genre and field and/or topic, are clearly important and have already been dealt with. When it comes to the language actually used, the stereotype is disappointingly vague, suggesting merely some kinds of lexical differences (principally involving the use of slang, swear-words, and possibly euphemisms) and in the most general terms, some differences in pronunciation and grammar (not going beyond the question of extent of conformity to some standard or prestige norm).

When one turns to the literature on male and female speech, however, one is not much further enlightened. The psychological literature is frequently linguistically naive and, like most of the psychological work relating to gender, fixated on difference. Archer and Lloyd (1982, pp.13−14) point out that the statistical techniques commonly employed in such research focus on the data of groups as wholes and allow one to ignore the range of variation **within** groups, which commonly indicates that males and females are more alike than they are different. They also suggest that the publication policy of psychology journals has meant that reports with statistically significant differences are more likely to be accepted for publication than those with no significant differences—and remind us that statistical significance has nothing to do with the magnitude of the difference but ony the likelihood of it having occurred purely by chance.

Much of the recent work on women's and men's language has been carried out by people whose interests are basically political rather than linguistic, some of whom have little sophistication in linguistic analysis and interpretation and others of whom do not seem to have felt the need to relate what they are doing to what anyone else in linguistics is doing. (See Philips, 1980, McConnell-Ginet, 1983.) McConnell-Ginet (1983, p.374) makes the two germane points that 'detailed descriptions of the linguistic structures actually used' are needed for comparability between studies and that the results of such studies need to be 'interpreted within some general theory of language'. In the concluding section of this review article, she gives some indications of what that general theory needs to take into account. Of particular interest are her observations of the value of Brown's and Levinson's work on politeness (Brown & Levinson, 1978; Brown, 1980) insofar as it uses 'a general theory of social relations' (albeit inadequate at the moment) 'in combination with detailed analysis of speech actions—of linguistic forms and their uses' (McConnell-Ginet, 1983, p.386). It is precisely towards this end that the final chapter will direct its attention.

The ⬤rd and final preliminary point that needs to be made concerns the question of the interpretation of differences between female and male speech. The crudest kind of interpretation would be to offer none at all, to simply assert that men and women speak differently because they are different. The GENDERLECT interpretation, which simply aggregates all features that have been identified in the speech of women and men and postulates separate 'women's' and 'men's' languages, is not much more sophisticated than this, even when this postulated separateness is seen as related to the different circumstances of men's and women's lives. The embarrassing fact is that women and men do not speak separate languages, that they all use the same linguistic resources, though undoubtedly with different frequencies in many cases. And, further, unless one can demonstrate how the interconnection between one's life and one's language use actually works, one is in effect saying no more than that men and women are different.

A considerable step in sophistication is taken by those who approach the question of interpretation by asking what more general social phenomena, other than gender itself, might play a role in determining the actual linguistic choices made. Here the work of O'Barr and his colleagues on language in the courtroom (O'Barr & Atkins, 1980; O'Barr, 1982) has been of importance in looking at the set of features originally identified as characteristic of women's speech by Robin Lakoff (1975) in terms of powerlessness, i.e. women (and some men) talk as they do because of their position of relative powerlessness both in the society as a whole and in the context of particular relationships.

Here again, however, one needs a socio-linguistic theory capable of relating in a motivated and explicit way the social phenomena of power and powerlessness (which will need to be rigorously defined) to the linguistic phenomena that mark or realise them. Further, although one understands the political motivation that has made an approach to explaining the characteristics of women's language in terms of men's power over women's lives extremely appealing to many feminists, such an approach only enables one to make sense of what happens when women are talking to men. As McConnell-Ginet points out, it 'sheds little light on how gender might function in woman–woman conversations' (1983, p. 384)—unless, presumably, if some of the same linguistic features as occur in woman–man conversations recur, one is prepared to invoke some kind of model of learned inflexible behaviour that is incapable of being sensitive to context. We know too much now, however, about the ways in which language is highly sensitive to context for any such approach to be tenable.

What is needed is an approach that models key aspects of context, both cultural and situational, as determining probabilistically (not absolutely) certain specifiable features of the language produced in actual situations. We don't need a 'grammar of style', at least in the terms proposed in Lakoff (1979) and cogently criticised by McConnell-Ginet (1983, esp. pp. 385–6), that uses '(super)grammatical rules' that are intended to generate what will actually be said. What is needed is what we might call a 'grammar of context', which sees the grammatical options open to speakers as present in the first place because of what speakers do with them, and therefore as sensitive to those uses. Before proceeding to an account of how such an approach might work in relation to the language of women and men, some description of the differences between men's and women's speech needs to be provided.

See the section 'Language and the making of meaning' in Chapter 1, pp. 6–11.

Differences between women's and men's speech

The first point that should be made is that the differences assumed or demonstrated in this section concern gender role (or social role mediated by gender) and not gender identity, which is largely conveyed by means that are outside the linguistic system.

Turning to linguistic differences between women and men, let us begin by noting that there do seem to be linguistic features that are stereotypically associated with men and women, that there is a large measure of agreement about the association of such features with one or the other gender, and that children learn to associate more and more of such features with the appropriate gender group over time (Edelsky, 1977). Table 5.1 summarises Edelsky's findings with respect to twelve linguistic items or structures (listed in isolation in the left-hand column), which were presented in sentences (each one twice but not together) to 244 subjects from four age groups (first-, third-, and sixth-grade children, and adults). The actual items/structures tested were selected on the basis of Lakoff (1973, 1975).

See Philips (1980, pp. 526–9) for an up-to-date overview. Among references she cites are Birdwhistell (1970, pp. 39–40) on kinesic display, Goffman (1976) on the implications of the poses used in advertisements – profusely illustrated; McConnell-Ginet (1978a) on intonation and responses to it: in particular that the greater variability in women's intonation patterns is taken as an indication of their inherent emotional instability. To which one should add Nancy Henley's aptly titled *Body Politics* (1977) − an excellent introduction to the whole range of non-linguistic modes of communication, focused on gender.

Table 5.1 Items stereotypically associated with women's and men's speech by four age groups

| Variable | Age groups | | | |
	First graders	Third graders	Sixth graders	Adults
Adorable	W	W*	W*	W*
Damn it	M*	M*	M*	M
Damn + Adjective	—	M*	M*	M
I'll be damned	—	M*	M*	M*
Oh dear	—	W*	W*	W*
My goodness	—	W	W*	W*
Won't you please	—	W	W*	W
Tag Question	—	M/W	W	W
So	—	—	W	W
Very	—	—	W	W
Just	—	—	W	W
Command	—	—	M	M/W

Note: W* = Female, high consensus; W = female, low consensus; M* = male, high consensus; M = male, low consensus: M/W = neutral: — = not meeting criteria.

Source: Edelsky (1977), p. 233

Edelsky's study is extremely interesting, not the least because of her finding that sixth-grade children in some cases exhibited a higher level of consensus than did adults in assigning a variable to one or other gender: it is ideologically predictable that children on the verge of adolescence stereotype to a greater extent than adults in the same community. This study is also interesting in that it demonstrates that one can identify stereotypic (indexical) linguistic features on the basis of introspection alone, as Lakoff did. Going further than fairly random lists of apparently unrelated linguistic phenomena is more difficult, particularly since the relevant features are going to differ only in frequency of occurrence: introspection is hardly likely to turn up meaningful numbers.

For surveys and overviews of differences see Bodine (1975a); Borker (1980); Haas (1979); Kramer et al. (1978); McConnell-Ginet (1980); Philips (1980); Smith (1979); Thorne & Henley (1975a); Thorne et al. (1983). Where no specific reference is found below, the source of the information will be in one or another of these papers.

In what follows, I have endeavoured to present a fairly comprehensive list of what is currently known about differences between women and men speaking English and to present what is known in some kind of rational order. The order is by linguistic stratum in the first instance (discourse, lexico-grammar, and phonology) and within the lexico-grammatical stratum, by rank (clause, group, word). (The discourse stratum has no rank scale and the phonological stratum will not be dealt with in sufficient detail to require specification of its rank scale.) This listing of linguistic features will be treated like a set of raw data insofar as it will be followed by a systemic-functional interpretation that ties together much of this data into meaningful patterns. This interpretation will then be used as the basis for the final chapter, connecting contextual and linguistic variables in a motivated way.

Discourse stratum

Interruption: men interrupt women and not vice versa in mixed-sex conversations.

Switching pause: White males have a longer pause after their turn than do White females in mixed-sex dyads. The pattern is the reverse for Black dyads (US data).

Topic choice: men may (and do) reject women's topic choices in mixed-sex conversation while women will talk on topics raised by men.

Back-channel noises: women use *mm hmm* significantly more than men, particularly in woman-to-woman conversations. Such noises, together with linguistic items such as *Yeah* and *I see*, function as signals that the communication channel remains open.

Speech function (speech act) choice and realisation: men use many more Commands than women and tend to realise them congruently by means of the mood choice Imperative. When women do use Commands, they are much more likely to realise them incongruently, e.g. by choosing Interrogative, especially modalised (*Would you mind shutting the door?*) or, even more incongruently, by using a Declarative clause (*I wonder if you would be so kind as to shut the door.*). The choice of these forms is often glossed as **politeness**—which often tends to obscure what is going on linguistically. The notion of congruent/incongruent realisation seems very useful.

See Brown & Levinson (1978), for an enlightening account of politeness phenomena in three unrelated languages.

Initiating conversations: women try to initiate conversation more often than men but succeed less often because of lack of male co-operation.

Lexico-grammatical stratum: grammar

Clause rank

Mood choices: these are most relevantly looked at in terms of the speech function they are realising. Much has been made in the literature, however, of TAGS, which will be dealt with here (i.e. the repetition at the end of a clause of the finite element, generally with reversed polarity, for example:

See speech function on the discourse stratum.

> We might come tomorrow, <u>mightn't we?</u>
> It's a nice day, <u>isn't it?</u>
> He can't do that, <u>can he?</u>

Tags: Lakoff (1975) claimed that women use them more than men, and subjects in several laboratory studies consistently attribute them to women, but observational studies have found either no difference or that men used them rather more than women.

Modality/modulation: commonly referred to as **hedges**, i.e. the variety of means by which one can say something a little short of indicating that something categorically is, or is not, the case. Includes MODALS (*would*, *might*, *must*, *ought*), modal adverbs (*probably*, *possibly*, *certainly*) and interpersonal metaphors (*I think*, *I suppose*, as in *I suppose I might be able to*).

See Dubois & Crouch (1976), who do not give any indication, however, of the extent of women's participation in the ongoing speech, i.e. the potential for tags to be used by women.

Women are supposed generally to use more 'hedges' than men, a part of the stereotype of tentativeness associated with their speech. Women are also said to use more 'super-polite' forms, that is, multiple modality, for example:

> I was <u>wondering</u> if you <u>could possibly just</u> do me a small favour, if you <u>wouldn't</u> mind.

Transitivity choices: process types and participant roles: there is some evidence (not entirely clear) that men and women may make different choices of process type (material, i.e. doing, by men, and mental or relational, i.e. thinking, feeling, and 'be-ing', by women) and hence different choices of participant role, (Actor and Goal, only available in material process clauses, Sensor and Phenomenon in mental process clauses, and various roles in relational clauses). The whole question of transitivity within a systemic-functional model is unfortunately too complex to go into here.

See Chapter 5, 'Clause as representation', in Halliday (1985).

Terms of address (vocatives): there is considerable evidence that different choices are made by and to men and women, relevant not only to the question of relative status or power but also to the question of social distance, with men assuming lesser distance between themselves and women. Address will be taken up in more detail in Chapter 6.

Sentence length: there is limited evidence that girls produce longer sentences than boys but that in adulthood the reverse may be true (Haas, 1979, pp. 618–9). What the significance of this may be is unclear: one would need to know what kinds of sentences were being produced by men and women to see what kinds of functional elements might be being elaborated or omitted.

Sentence completeness: Jesperson (1922) thought that women left sentences incomplete more often than men—Haas (1979, p.618) suggests this may be because women get interrupted more often!

Direct quotation: women are supposed to use direct quotation rather than paraphrase. O'Barr and Atkins (1980) include this as one of their indicators of powerless language, but because of the rules regarding hearsay evidence in a court of law, not many instances were collected in their data. (All were, however, produced by women and none by men.)

Group rank

Nominal group (There is no evidence I am aware of concerning verbal or adverbial groups.)

Adjective frequency: several studies found that girls used more adjectives than boys in both speech and writing, but no differences were found in one study of college students' writing.

Adjective type: considerable evidence that women use evaluative (attitudinal) adjectives more than men (e.g. *wonderful*, *darling*, and *gorgeous*). This seems to be related to the pervasive stereotype of women functioning in terms of feeling or emotion rather than rationality or logic. Where men do use evaluative adjectives, they tend to use different items from women.

Adjectives of approximation (*about*, *around*): women are claimed to use these more than men and there is some evidence to confirm this.

Intensifiers (sub-modification: *so*, *very*, etc.): women are said to use these more than men.

Possessive construction: Haas (1979, pp.621–2) refers to one study that found that fifth-grade boys used this more than girls. No details are provided as to what kind of possessives (*my* or *your/hers/his* or more elaborate constructions such as *my father's* or *Ms Peterson's*).

Word rank

Reduplicated forms: women are reputed to use more reduplicated adjectival forms—Key (1975, p.75) cites *itsy-bitsy* and *teeny-tiny*. Reduplicated hypocoristic forms (pet forms) of personal names, such as *Ally-Bally* and *Stevie-Weave* (the added or changed initial consonant in the second element is characteristic of reduplicated forms in English) are also more used by women than men—they would be seen by many people as part of 'baby-talk' and hence inappropriate for male use.

Lexico-grammatical stratum: lexis

Field range: women and men seem to include different lexical sets ain their total repertoires, depending on the range and kinds of field they are involved in. Lakoff's best-known example is that of colour terms, which she suggests women have a more differentiated command of than men.

Slang: men are generally supposed to use more slang than women. Men's greater use of slang is generally interpreted as indicative of greater bonding (or solidarity) between males than between females in English-speaking societies. Slang also happens to occur in relaxed speech—it may be the case that male linguists haven't had much access to relaxed female conversation!

However, see Keesing's (1982) collection, subtitled *Slang of Australian Women and Families*.

Swearing: even more than slang, this has been regarded as men's territory.

Euphemism: women have a consistent reputation for being less prepared to call a spade a spade then men, especially with reference to sexual matters and bodily functions.

Politeness markers (*please*, *thanks*): women are said to use these more than men.

Phonological stratum

Phonological variants: where there are variant pronunciations, women tend to a greater extent than men to use the form with higher prestige, e.g. to pronounce participal forms ending in *-ing* with /ŋ/ rather than /n/ (the folklinguistic characterisation of the latter choice as 'dropping the g' is quite erroneous: the difference is merely a matter of two kinds of nasal consonant, one of which (the velar) happens to be standard or prestigious in words of this kind). Another example of women choosing a prestige form is the fact that far fewer women than men speak with a broad Australian accent and far more women than men with a cultivated accent. Women are not always more linguistically conservative than men, however: they can be in the vanguard of linguistic change. The most recent picture is even more complex, with women seen as having a wider spread of variation than men (Kroch, 1978; Horvath, 1985).

Kramer et al. (1978, p. 639) note that phonological differences are the best documented.

See Mitchell & Delbridge (1965) and Horvath.

See Labov (1972b, pp.301–4); Nichols (1980).

Intonation: women's intonational tones are said to be:

> more dynamic than men's, displaying wider ranges of pitches, more frequent and rapid shifts in pitch, and more frequently ending with a nonfalling terminal than men's.
>
> (McConnell-Ginet, 1978a, p. 555)

There is some experimental verification of these suggested characteristics including, in the case of the last feature (the non-falling terminal, sometimes referred to as the high rising terminal (HRT) or—erroneously—as question intonation), Australian data indicating that men are significant users, accounting for around 40 per cent of the examples in the corpus examined (Guy et al., 1982; Guy & Vonwiller, 1984). This work is also important in that the meaning of this contour in Australian English seems to be 'to seek verification of the listener's comprehension' (Guy & Vonwiller, 1984, p.4) rather than the self-effacement and deference that Lakoff attributes to women using this form (1975, p.17).

Finally, outside the phonological stratum as such, but relevant to perceptions of men's and women's speech, is the question of FUNDAMENTAL FREQUENCY (basically, voice pitch). It is widely assumed that this is largely a biological matter, with the post-pubertal lengthening and thickening of the vocal cords of males producing deeper voices on the whole than those of females. Several kinds of evidence indicate that matters are not quite as simple as that. The work of Sachs and her colleagues demonstrates that pitch may be in part learned, as part of gender role, rather than being simply a product of biology. Lieberman (1967) found that infants of ten months and thirteen months shifted the direction of the fundamental frequency of their vocalisations depending on whether they were interacting with their father or their mother, suggesting that the pitch–gender association may be learned extremely early.

See Sachs (1975).

Interpreting the differences systemically

In systemic-functional terms, what are we to make of all this ignoring phonology and focusing on discourse and lexico-grammar? The model assumed is that of Martin (1985b) with the central systems noted for the two relevant strata (phonology omitted). See Figure 5.1.

Figure 5.1   Central systems in two linguistic strata

discourse	lexico-grammar
CONVERSATIONAL STRUCTURE CONJUNCTION REFERENCE LEXICAL COHESION	TRANSITIVITY THEME MOOD LEXIS group and word systems

Source: adapted from Martin (1985b), Figure 1, p. 249

On the discourse stratum, the main system implicated is CONVERSATIONAL STRUCTURE, which includes both **exchange structure** and **speech function**. Exchange structure involves the question of who is/is not primary knower or primary actor. The roles are frequently either assigned to males by females—'Ask him about himself!'—or abrogated by males by means of interrupting females to take over the role of primary knower. Speech function choices, together with the grammatical choices from the mood network that realise them, are both significant: the more frequent use by males of Command, realised through Imperative mood, contrasted with the infrequent choice by females of Command and the tendency to realise such choices incongruently, for example by modalised Interrogatives, says a great deal about institutionalised power and gender—and of course is significant in relation to the speech exchange roles taken up by females and males.

The other systems on this stratum may also be implicated to a lesser extent. The folk stereotype of women's talk 'jumping all over the place', and 'never following an idea through' would seem to implicate lexical cohesion. Presumably some of the effect noted in the stereotype is due to women being more liable to interruption (and thus not getting a chance to follow an idea through) and being generally more attentive to their addressee's topics and conversational needs than their own. This would be an interesting issue to investigate.

There is a possibility that the other discourse systems, REFERENCE and CONJUNCTION, are also implicated both in relation to the field/topic mobility stereotype and also in relation to exchange structure: who refers to whose talk and who makes internal conjunctive links, for example *You mean . . .*

At the lexico-grammatical stratum, the main system implicated is clearly mood in terms of actual mood choices, tags, modality/modulation, and vocation (address). There are some indications that the TRANSITIVITY system is implicated, which would make sense, given that participant roles can be seen in part as experientialised versions of actual conversational roles. THEME has not been investigated. Below clause rank, modification in the nominal group and hypocoristic forms at word rank would seem to be important.

An overall pattern in the systems sensitive to gender is clearly discernible: the primary systems implicated are those that realise interpersonal meaning of various kinds, and secondarily affected are those systems realising experiential meaning. We now turn our attention back to the connection between grammatical choices and contextual variables posited earlier—the register—metafunction 'hook-up'. The final chapter will offer a formalisation of those aspects of social relations that seem relevant to interpersonal choices and will attempt to make the hook-up explicit.

For examples of what can be done by investigating ideology in whole texts, but not with reference to gender, see Martin (1986c); Fowler et al. (1979), especially the papers by Tony Trew.

Chapter 6
Social relations through grammar

The semiotics of social relations

The most influential piece of work in explicating the relationship between linguistic phenomena and the world of social relations has
undoubtedly been Brown and Gilman's classic paper, 'The pronouns
of power and solidarity' (Brown & Gilman, 1960). In investigating the
use of pronouns of address in European languages that have a choice
(*tu/vous* in French, *du/ihr/sie* in German, etc.), Brown and Gilman found
that the choice depended on one's relationship to one's addressee on
two dimensions: a vertical **power** dimension and a horizontal **solidarity**
dimension. Most of the subsequent work on pronouns of address in
languages other than those investigated by Brown and Gilman, and the
work of Brown himself, in conjunction with Ford, on address in
American English (Brown & Ford, 1964), has used this two-dimensional
model.

My own systemic-functional work on address in English, which
includes a detailed account of 'pet'-forms (hypocoristic forms) of names,
together with nicknames and insulting or affectionate nominals (Poynton,
1984; in preparation), suggests that three dimensions are needed for
an adequate characterisation of the contextual variable **tenor** rather than
Brown and Gilman's two. Two of these dimensions are a consequence
of splitting Brown and Gilman's solidarity dimension into two,
distinguishing between a social distance or intimacy dimension called
CONTACT and an attitudinal dimension concerned with attitude or
emotion towards addressee (or towards the field of discourse) called
AFFECT. The third dimension remains POWER. These three dimensions
are formalised systemically in the following network (see Figure 6.1).

It should be noted that systems here on the whole are to be taken
as representing clines, or continua, rather than discrete choices. **Power**
ranges from equal to unequal, with the basis of that power deriving from
at least one (and maybe more than one) of the factors specified: **force**
involves physical superiority; **authority** is a function of socially-
legitimated inherently unequal role relationships such as parent—child,
teacher—child, employer—employee, or ruler—ruled; **status** is a matter
of relative ranking with respect to some unevenly distributed but socially-

76

Figure 6.1   Register plane: tenor

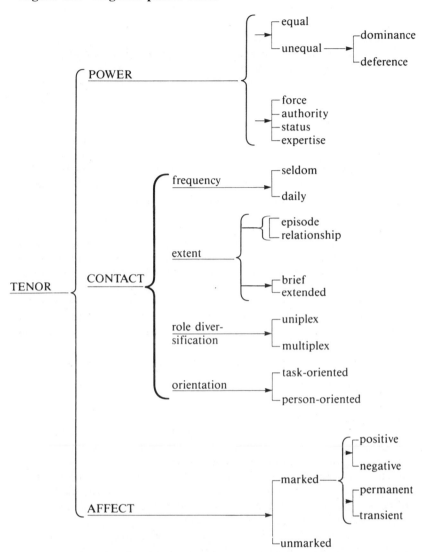

desirable object or standing or achievement, e.g. wealth, profession/occu-pation, level of education, hereditary status, location of residence, overseas travel; **expertise** is a matter of the extent to which an individual possesses knowledge or skill, e.g. the expert knitter compared with the novice, the nuclear physicist with the high school student beginning to study physics. It will be noted that **age**, **gender**, and **race**, familiar sources of power inequality, are not mentioned. This is because all of these are seen as matters of ideology. As we will see in the case of gender, all three dimensions of social relations are affected by it, so that gender must be outside this network and not part of it.

The **contact** dimension has to take a number of factors into consideration: the **frequency** of interaction and the **extent** in time (of both the relationship itself and also individual communicative episodes) of the contact; the extent of the **role-diversification**—whether people relate to one another in one capacity only, e.g. customer and newspaper-seller, or in a wide range of contexts, e.g. lover/friend/co-participant in hobby/political ally etc.; and finally whether the **orientation** of the inter-action is primarily towards persons or towards tasks.

The third dimension, **affect**, differs from the other two in that it may be absent, whereas an interaction can always be located on a cline somewhere between equal and unequal power, and somewhere between greatest and least contact (lumping all the component variables in together, for convenience). Whether or not affect is marked will depend on what kind of power and contact choices have been made: in particular, the subordinate in an unequal power relationship is less likely to choose affect than the superior (lest offence be given or taken), while in interactions characterised in terms of greatest contact, i.e. intimacy, affect is expected (specifically, positive affect: negative affect between intimates, e.g. antagonism between siblings, is culturally frowned on, though it occurs quite commonly). If affect is present, the primary choice is between **positive** and **negative**, and in terms of either the relationship as a whole or an individual episode. For example, a fight between lovers, or a conversation between a professor and a student after the football grand final won by the team they both barrack for, may both be characterised in terms of transient affect, the usual choices being marked positive in the case of the lovers, and unmarked in the case of the professor—student dyad.

The linguistic realisation of social relations

Now comes the crucial question of getting from this tenor network on the register plane to the various systems on the language plane (discourse, lexico-grammatical, and phonological systems). First, however, a word about the notion of **choice**. When terms within systems are referred to as choices or options, this is not to be interpreted as meaning that speakers make a conscious and deliberate choice from the total range of possibilities: most of the linguistic choices actually made are made quite unconsciously—and no single person controls the full system of the language anyway, only certain ranges of choices. The notion of choice, then, is a matter of the options that the language as a system makes available for realising meanings and, in the case of contextual variables, which the society makes available. It is certainly true that some of the linguistic options may be ones that speakers have some aware-ness of, and hence control over. It is also true that some individuals may 'choose' to present themselves in certain guises, which can be inter-preted in terms of particular configurations of tenor options rather than other possible configurations. In this case such speakers cannot be said to be 'choosing' the tenor options themselves. One does not 'choose' equal power or task-oriented close contact or positive affect: these are elements of the situation itself, only in some historical sense to be seen as a consequence of decisions made by the participants in that situation (to take that job, marry that person, get involved in that project).

The options of the tenor network are to be understood, then, as those culturally meaningful alternatives in relating to people that are manifested, or realised, in culturally significant communicative behaviour. Much of this behaviour will be linguistic, but one should not underestimate the importance of non-verbal means of communication in negotiating relationships, particularly with reference to gender.

See Henley (1977).

In moving between tenor and language, we know that the principal linguistic systems involved are interpersonal: at clause rank involving mood, modality and modulation, and vocation (the system of address). These systems are utilised to make the kinds of meaning that are regarded as culturally appropriate for different kinds of social relations. Thus the use of modalised or modulated clauses rather than ones with definite positive or negative polarity (something **might** be the case rather than definitely is or is not the case) is commonly dependent on whether one is subordinate or superior to one's addressee. The use of clauses with certain kinds of ellipsis (certain elements of clause structure not realised, e.g. *Want a drink?* rather than *Do you want a drink?*) or with certain kinds of presuming or non-specific reference (e.g. greeting a partner arriving home, having had an important interview that day, with *Well, how was it?* rather than the more specific *Well, how did the interview go?*) is generally dependent on how well one knows the person one is talking to, i.e. is a function of contact.

Each of the three tenor dimensions seems to activate somewhat different sets of linguistic choices and to do so with characteristic patterning of the realisations. Such patterning can be structural or interactional. For the power dimension, the characteristic realisational pattern is interactional, in terms of the extent of RECIPROCITY of the linguistic choices made. For the dimensions of contact and affect, the characteristic realisational patterns are structural, in terms of what I shall call the principles of PROLIFERATION and AMPLIFICATION. In saying a little about each of these realisational principles below, I shall merely mention the major linguistic choices involved, but Table 6.1 presents a somewhat more detailed summary of what we currently know about which linguistic choices are activated by which tenor choice.

Power is realised primarily in terms of linguistic choices on the discourse stratum and at clause rank within lexico-grammar, with the equality or inequality of interactants indicated by the extent of **reciprocity** of those choices. The greater the equality between interactants, the more likely they are to behave linguistically in parallel or symmetrical ways: equals have an equal right to interrupt one another, to nominate new topics, to take on the role of primary knower or actor, to be definite rather than tentative, to reciprocate address terms that are contextually appropriate for the extent of contact and affect involved. Conversely, the greater the inequality between interactants, the more likely it is that their linguistic behaviour will be non-reciprocal: superiors have rights to interrupt, to nominate topics, to be definite, etc. that subordinates do not have. And superiors can invoke sanctions of various kinds if subordinates fail to observe what is regarded as an appropriate level of non-reciprocity by 'taking over the conversation' (interrupting or by asking rather than answering questions), by 'being familiar' (using a name-form they have not been invited to use, or by using slang or ellipsis), or by 'being rude' (failing to include appropriate politeness markers even though the superior may use none).

Contact is realised primarily within lexico-grammar, particularly in terms of lexis but also at all ranks of the grammar: clause, group, word, and morpheme (minimal unit of meaning). Here the extent of the contact is realised in terms of **proliferation**, or the range of options available. Generally the greater the contact, the larger the range of options, and the less the contact, the smaller the range (to the point where fleeting contacts with strangers or people one barely knows are commonly quite ritualised, hence small-talk about the weather in English-speaking societies). Affect is realised primarily at group rank and below within lexico-grammar and also, most importantly, on the phonological stratum in terms of variation in intonation, rhythm, rate of speech, etc. Here the relevant realisational principle seems to be **amplification**, generally achieved by the repetition of identical or functionally equivalent elements of structure, increases in the strength of the affect being realised in terms of amount of repetition as well as choice of actual item. Thus someone really pleased about something might say:

It's great! It's super! It's terrific! It's fantastically, unbelievably bloody wonderful! (with pace increasing and pitch rising)

and someone really angry with someone else might castigate that person in the following terms:

You filthy, rotten, lousy, mongrel cur!

Table 6.1 sets out some of the principle systems that realise the three dimensions of tenor.

The politics of address

At this stage, let us take up the issue of address, which undoubtedly provides the most elaborated resource for the linguistic realisation of social relations, including those between women and men. It will not be possible within the space available to give a comprehensive account of address in relation to gender, merely to take up some key issues in relation to each of the tenor dimensions of power, contact, and affect.

Firstly, as far as power is concerned, it has often been observed that address between males and females in public contexts is asymmetrical: male bosses may be addressed as *Mr O'Halloran*, *Mr Nguyen*, etc. by their female secretaries or junior staff, but address them by their first name in return, even when the woman is considerably older than the man. Or, given the widespread (and even, in some companies, mandatory) use of first name as the basic unmarked address choice, women may address men who are their superiors or their peers by first name, but be addressed in return by some conventional endearment such as *dear*, *sweetheart*, or *love*. Wolfson and Manes (1980) found a related asymmetry in service encounters, with endearments used by both male and female shop assistants to women customers but never to men, who were commonly addressed as *Sir* if any address term was used. In Australia, one finds the considerably less formal *mate* used between males in many kinds of service encounter, especially when the transaction

Stratum/Rank	Power	Contact	Affect
Discourse	**Conversational structure:** turn-taking, including length of turn, interruption; primary/secondary actor/doer status; speech function choice.		
	Lexical cohesion: who controls strings (field/topic choice).		
	Reference: who refers to whom, and to whose discourse, and how. Homophora to include/exclude, e.g. name-dropping.		
	Conjunction: who controls/reformulates internal conjunction, e.g. *Do you mean . . .?, So then?*		
Lexico-grammar: Grammar			
Clause	**Mood:** Extent of congruence in relation to speech function choice.		**Exclamatives**
	Presence and extent of modulation/modality.	**Ellipsis**	
	◄——— **Tags** ———►		
	Vocation: reciprocity	**Vocation:** range of choices	**Vocation:** attitudinals; amplified structures.
Nominal group			Extent and kind of modification: amplified structures; intensification.
Word		Truncation (clipping). Suffixation.	Suffixation. Reduplication. Infixing (only with expletives in English, e.g. *kanga-bloodyroo*)
Lexis	Technical lexis.	Slang.	Swearing. Attitudinal lexis.
Phonology		Elision.	Rhythm. Rate. Pitch.

81

involves a 'male' product such as petrol, auto parts, hardware, paint, and particularly alcohol (either in the bar or the bottle-shop). *Mate* is also used in more neutral contexts such as post offices, milk bars, and the local paper shop. Such public male usage is often reciprocal and is best seen as a conventionalised marker of Australian egalitarian ideology, which historically has been exclusively male (Ward, 1958).

Given that the vast majority of women work in lower status jobs and are more likely than not to have male superiors, the fact of non-reciprocal use in work contexts is not surprising. What is interesting is the nature of the asymmetry, particularly when the same choices to women occur in other contexts. It would seem that women, like children, can be addressed in public with conventionalised intimate forms to a far greater extent than is permissible for men. (There would seem to be social dialect differences here, which permit some women to use endearments more freely to males at work or in service encounters. Such differences have not been investigated for class/socio-economic status, though Wolfson and Manes (1980) collected data from different geographical areas in the USA.)

The choice of endearments to women in public contexts can be linked with the fact that even when reciprocal use of first names occurs between men and women (or girls and boys), the form of that choice tends to be different. If the full form of the name is not used (*Robert, Tamara, Jason, Katharine*, etc), then adult males will generally be addressed with a monosyllabic truncated form of the full name (*Rob/Bob, Jase, Chris* from *Christopher*, etc.) whereas the form usually used to females, adults as well as children, will be one with the diminutive suffix *-y* (sometimes spelt *-ie*): *Tammy, Kathy, Chrissie* from *Christine/Christina*, etc. These suffixed forms, along with other diminutive suffixes such as *-kin(s)* and *-poo(s)*, are commonly used to children of both sexes, but boys come to see them, sometimes at a very early age, as 'girls' names' and reject them. Thus four-year-old *Robbie* at fourteen insists on *Rob* and six-year-old *Nicholas* has already rejected *Nicky* in favour of *Nick* or the full form *Nicholas*.

The relevant tenor dimension here is **contact**: the use of diminutive or hypocoristic forms of names is a matter of increases in intimacy. The process is most clearly seen in the progression of a couple falling in love from the most commonly used forms of their respective names, when they first meet, to a variety of pet-forms of those names (including quite elaborate constructions involving up to five suffixes, e.g. *Anniekins, Mikeypoodles* (Poynton, 1984), plus private nicknames and a good selection of endearments as the relationship develops. The proliferation principle is clearly seen in operation here in opening up a morphological resource for forming diminutives in English that particular individuals may not previously have had much occasion to make use of, leading to the production of a variety of forms all having substantially the same meaning of marking intimacy.

The relationship between name choices and contact can be seen very clearly also in the reverse direction, away from intimacy, in the set of name forms that are addressed to a child depending on how she or he stands in the favour of parents, from *Katiekindlekins* when she's being utterly sweet and adorable, to *Katie-K* or just *Katie* for everyday affectionate usage, to *Kate* (for calling her or when doing jobs together) to *Katharine* (when someone isn't too happy with her) to *Katharine Pirona* (when she's done something pretty bad), to *Katharine Luisa Pirona* (for really bad news). (The example is an invented one, but the pattern is one that parents and teachers recognise, once it has been pointed out.)

If one now asks why women retain the more intimate forms into adulthood to a greater extent than is the case for men (think of all the women you know who are called *Judy, Suzie, Jenny, Margie, Libby, Rosie,* etc. compared with the number of men called *Bernie, Tommy, Normie, Billy,* etc.), the answer would seem to be that women are culturally defined as more contact-able than men: it is assumed that relations between males and females will be on the basis of intimacy. Such an interpretation makes sense of the persistent tendency for English words referring to women to acquire sexual connotations (compare the present range of meaning of *master* and *mistress*, of *madam* and *sir*): contact-able comes to mean sexually available. It makes sense of the fact that the not extensive repertoire of diminutive-forming resources in English (contrasted with the rich resources in languages such as Russian or Spanish) has come to be substantially gender-marked and in such a way that 'feminine' forms demean, belittle, and trivialise at the same time as they feminise. The process is very apparent with feminine words suffixed in *-ess* or *-ette*, examined above. It is less obvious with name forms, for two reasons. One is that, because in Western cultures intimacy (greater contact) is automatically associated with positive affect, the use of suffixed forms of personal names can be claimed to be an indication of friendliness, or affection: as a matter of affect and not of contact, much less power. Many males believe this to be the case and are genuinely puzzled and even upset when accused of belittling or trivialising women by using diminutive forms. The only possible response would seem to be that some things, in this case the cultural functions of the linguistic system, are 'larger than personal benevolence' (as Gayati Chakravorty Spivak noted with respect to history and the well-meaning individual, in a public lecture at the University of Sydney, 1 August 1984.)

The second reason for diminutive name forms not always being seen as belittling is particularly relevant to speakers of Australian English, many of whom, particularly males, use a large number of words with the characteristic 'diminutive' *-y* ending in everyday casual conversation: *tinny* (can of beer), *barbie* (barbecue), *bookie* (bookmaker), *footy* (football), *carbie* (carburettor of a car), *trannie* (transistor radio), *hankie* (handkerchief), *mozzie* (mosquito), *pokies* (poker-machines), *prezzie* (present), *pozzie* (position), *wharfie* ('wharf', i.e. waterside worker), etc. The use of such forms seems clearly related to contact, occurring in and/or being used to create relatively relaxed informal interaction—the egalitarian mateship theme again, in fact. None of these forms have any hint of a trivialising or demeaning flavour, though other items seen as baby-talk or specifically associated with women may. For males the *-y* suffix on everyday lexical items is probably best characterised along with the *-o* suffix, which is also widely used (*rego* for registration, *compo* for compensation, etc.), as a familiarity marker. In address between males, however, the -y suffix, along with a number of other hypocoristic suffixes used in name forms, commonly occurs with the last name rather than the first name (*Hawkie*, *Bondy*, *Lawsie*, etc. alongside forms such as *Thommo*, *Singo*, *Hoges*, etc.). Such forms would seem to achieve a nice balance between friendly camaraderie on the one hand and maintaining a certain distance—standing well back from real intimacy—on the other: asserting at one and the same time mateship and freedom from any conceivable homosexual 'taint'. This is clearly yet another manifestation of the male tendency to interpret intimacy only in sexual terms, commented on earlier with respect to cultural attitudes towards women (manifested in another form in common reactions to the shared sleeping and/or bathing arrangements of other cultures).

It is not then the choice *per se* of the -y suffix in address to females that is the problem: it is the lack of parallelism with its use to males and the cultural implications of the difference. Women may be addressed more intimately than is appropriate for males, not only with respect to name forms but in a variety of other ways. Endearments are commonly used publicly to women, who may also find themselves addressed by complete strangers in terms of their physical appearance (*gorgeous*, *blondie*, *sexy-legs*, etc.) and addressed or referred to purely as sexual objects (either as people, albeit of little value: *tart*, *slut*, *whore*, *moll*, etc.; or merely as their own sexual organs: *pussy*, *cunt*, and the metaphoric *slut-box*).

In investigating the language of derogation in English—one lexical resource for realising affect (negative in this case)—one striking fact is that there is a quite extensive lexis of derogatory terms for women **as women** that is not paralleled by a set denigrating men **as men**. Men can be castigated for their moral failings (*bludger*, *no-hoper*, *piss-artist*), their sexual preferences (*faggot*, *fairy*, *poofter*), their intellectual short-comings (*drongo*, *dope*, *fuck-wit*), their incompetence or uncouthness (*yobbo*, *oaf*, *hoon* (also used in other senses)), and in more generally negative terms by referring to them as animals (*animal*, *mongrel*, *swine*), as body products or genitalia (female being more offensive) (*shit*, *fart*, *prick*, *cunt*), or simply as the all-purpose *bastard*, which has only recently largely lost its implied denigration of women, as the stigma attached to illegitimacy has lessened. It has taken the women's movement of the 1960s and 1970s to invent terms such as (*male*) *chauvinist* (*pig*) and *MCP*, in order to be able to refer negatively to males as males, particularly with respect to their attitudes and behaviour towards women.

Such a selection of issues concerning address as has been dealt with in the last few pages should serve to give some idea of what a rich field it is in relation to gender.

For further reading see Hopper et al. (1981); Kramer (1975); McConnell-Ginet (1978b); Poynton (1981, 1982, 1984 in preparation); Wolfson & Manes (1980).

Tenor and the ideology of gender

Some general observations on tenor in relation to gender now seem in order. Firstly, with respect to power it would seem that men are culturally legitimated as powerful and women not. The consequences of this are that relations between males are between those who are seen, and who see themselves, in terms of power. Power, or control, can be achieved in a number of ways, and success in its pursuit can be attested by wealth, political or social position, sporting or artistic achievement, the size of a business empire (legitimate or criminal), and in sheer destructiveness, in hurt done to people and damage to the world we inhabit: the obscenity of war, torture, and forced labour in the service of repressive political regimes, sexual exploitation of women and children for financial gain, annihilation of native people, denuding of natural landscapes, pollution of rivers and lakes. With all that at stake, men can see one another as accomplices or as rivals—or a little of both, which makes more sense of how males learn to organise their lives to realise appropriately masculine values of contact and affect. Women, on the other hand, are not legitimated in terms of power, hence relations between women and men in general (whatever the range of variation in individual relationships) are culturally defined as between powerful and powerless and this shows up linguistically in a variety of ways. Relations between women are not really allowed for in the model of social organisation that has controlled social practice for so long, since women have been defined as social beings within that model only in relation to men. Women are having to create new patterns of relating to one another, as well as legitimating those patterns that do have a history but which were so often not taken seriously by either men or women: the day-to-day interaction of women as neighbours, as mothers of children, as organisers for schools and other public facilities, as consumers, as listeners.

In terms of contact, women are culturally defined as contact-able, as are children. Thus though women in terms of power are private persons, in terms of contact they are very much public persons: to be looked at, commented on, assessed, approached for sexual favours, harassed if they don't provide them and, in the act that is the most extreme assertion of the cultural availability of all women, raped. Relations between men in terms of contact can be friendly (they are accomplices) but not too close (they are also rivals—and intimacy is culturally feminine, not masculine). Relations between women in terms of contact have until the very recent past been conducted by many without either camaraderie or real intimacy, since women too defined themselves in relation to males and saw other women as potential rivals. For many women, however, both in the past and present, the friendship of women has provided both camaraderie and intimacy. Whereas intimacy for males in English-speaking societies is largely sexual, this is not necessarily so for women, who have found support of many different kinds in close relations with mothers, sisters, daughters, and friends of different ages.

In terms of affect, the situation is perhaps even more complicated than for power and contact. To start with, the general Western ideological preference is for the logical and rational, rather than the emotional, i.e. affect is seen as culturally suspect. However, some emotions are more understandable and justifiable than others. It is possible to exhibit *righteous anger*, for instance. And this is very revealing because anger seems related to power, resulting either from frustration at one's inability to get people or things to go the way one wants them to go or resentment at being on the receiving end of someone else's exercise

Brown's observations on the greater social distance between women than between men in the Mayan community she did her field-work among are thought-provoking in terms of Western societies (Brown, 1980, pp.129–31).

of power of one kind or another. There are other negative emotional states that seem related to power: *contempt* and *disgust* are experienced by those who see themselves as in possession of some kind of ethical superiority (power) while *distress*, *fear*, and *shame* would seem to be reactions experienced in response to actions or events outside the control of the experiencer (or only affecting themselves, in the case of shame). The pattern of evaluation would seem to be that emotions that involve the exercise of power are respected (though one may wince at or disagree with the consequences) while emotion shown from a powerless position, or that proceeds from a response to situations, rather than an attempt to control them, is less valued. This latter category of course includes such positive emotions as *excitement*, *enjoyment*, and *surprise*.

It comes as no surprise then that it is culturally acceptable for men to display the 'powerful' emotions, especially anger, but not for women and children to do so: men can be *righteously angry*, but women merely *lose their tempers* and children *throw tantrums*. Even in their relations with children, women's anger can be seen as ineffective and as illegitimate. Women may display all the 'response' emotions, however, and thereby demonstrate their inferiority as human beings.

See the discussion on women and power in the classroom in Chapter 2, pp. 29–31.

The price paid by people of each gender for maintaining this particular ideological dichotomy would seem extraordinarily high: paid in an undeveloped capacity to respond and feel the 'softer' emotions by males, no doubt contributing to the aggressiveness and destructiveness of many; paid most notably in the depression of all those women who learned too well to repress their anger. And paid by all those women and men who, for one reason or another, failed to conform, to learn what they were supposed to learn about being male and female, but who nevertheless knew what it was they were supposed to have learned and that they had failed—or who somehow escaped that knowledge but not the social opprobrium that was the result of their deficiency. And the price paid by the whole society for the wasted talents of women and men, and the talents wasted in war: the lives lost, the bodies maimed, the psyches crippled, the relationships destroyed, the evidence of human skill and artistry erased, the earth laid waste, all in the name of men showing themselves to be men.

Epilogue
So where do we go from here?

The basic argument of the preceding chapters has been that women and men as groups tend to make different selections at all linguistic levels from phonology to genre. Such selections are to be understood as realising, and hence perpetuating, an ideological opposition between male and female that maintains that the two are different in specifiable ways and which validates the male and his activities as of great importance and value and the female and her activities as of lesser importance and value. The ideology functions as a legitimating mechanism for a particular kind of social organisation in which women and men do not participate on equal terms because they grow up learning to use the same language in different ways for different ends, and as a consequence of this to see themselves as different. Not Descartes' 'I think, therefore I am' (*cogito, ergo sum*) but 'I speak, therefore I am': I can only mean the meanings that I am allowed to make.

These overall differences can be referred to as SPEECH STYLES (see Maltz & Borker, 1982) or, preferably, as CODING ORIENTATIONS, after Bernstein's work on the relationship between social structure and the range of meanings available to members of different social classes (see Bernstein, 1971, 1973, 1975).

The link between social structure and what one can mean is the crucial one for gender as it seems to be for class, and both involve an unequal distribution of power. In terms of the distribution of political, social, and economic power, one needs to be able to talk about both class or power-based codes (ruling-class versus ruled-class(es) perhaps) and about gender-based codes. These will have certain things in common, since power is involved in both, but will also differ considerably, since different ideologies lie behind them.

In terms of gender, let us refer to the male **controlling code** and the female **responding code**, where males aim to control things, events, and most crucially people; and females show much more responsiveness to things, events, and particularly people. The consequences of such a difference in overall orientation are the continued resistance to the inclusion of women in access to real power and the continued marginalisation of those men who are not interested in power or control.

There would seem to be four options for the future:

See Spender (1982) for a comprehensive and devastating account of this process.

1. Leave things as they are—remembering that gains for women have often been lost in the past when social circumstances changed.
2. Teach women the male controlling code, which some have undoubtedly learned very successfully. But do we really want a whole society oriented in this way?
3. Teach men the female responding code, and again many males do function in this way. The problem here is that as long as social organisation is posited on power and control, one will have only limited success in teaching males to exclude themselves from such control, thereby marginalising themselves.
4. Blow the whistle: keep naming the ideology and particularly the practices that realise and sustain it, so that people can no longer say: 'I didn't mean . . .', 'I didn't know . . .', 'You're imagining things', 'You're making a mountain out a molehill', or simply make jokes about the whole thing—what Bev Roberts calls 'jocular sexism', referring to the practice, especially among media commentators, of 'the deliberate use of sexist terms but with an emphasis suggesting humour or irony—"I'm putting this word in quotes so you won't think I really mean it"'(Roberts, 1984, p.13).

A hopeful sign is the fact that the ideology of gender has become partially visible, as a consequence of social change; the traditional coding orientations are now out of step with some aspects of contemporary reality. But there is enormous resistance to be overcome from those to whom exposing ideology **as** ideology is truly shocking and outrageous, since for them ideology is **truth**, and to question it is to question the whole foundation of their world. And there are institutionalised interests that may or may not be themselves ideologically committed to traditional notions of gender whose interests are served by their perpetuation: much of contemporary consumer production and selling depends upon the continuation of certain conceptions of gender in order to make certain products saleable.

Challenging the ideology of gender then is about much more than objecting to a few sexist words and actions: it is about considering the kind of world that we all, women and men alike, might want to live in.

References

Archer, J., & Lloyd, B., *Sex and Gender* (Penguin, Harmondsworth, 1982).

Ariès, P., *Centuries of Childhood: A Social History of Family Life*, Childhood in Society, (Penguin, Harmondsworth, 1973).

Barnes, D., *From Communication to Curriculum* (Penguin, Harmondsworth, 1976).

Bate, B.A., 'Generic man, invisible woman: Language, thought, and social change', *University of Michigan Papers in Women's Studies* 2(1), 1976, pp. 2−13.

Berger, P.L., & Luckmann, T., *The Social Construction of Reality: A Treatise in the Sociology of Knowledge* (Penguin, Harmondsworth, 1966).

Bernstein, B., *Class, Codes and Control*, vol. 1, *Theoretical Studies towards a Sociology of Language*, Primary Socialisation, Language and Education (Routledge & Kegan Paul, London, 1971).

Bernstein, B., *Class, Codes and Control*, vol. 2 *Applied Studies towards a Sociology of Language*, Primary Socialisation, Language and Education (Routledge & Kegan Paul, London, 1973).

Bernstein, B., *Class, Codes and Control*, vol. 3 *Towards a Theory of Educational Transmissions*, Primary Socialisation, Language and Education (Routledge & Kegan Paul, London, 1975).

Birdwhistell, R., *Kinesics and Context: Essays on Body-motion Communication* (Penguin, Harmondsworth, 1970).

Bodine, A., 'Sex differentiation in language', in Thorne & Henley (1975b), 1975a, pp. 130−151.

Bodine, A., 'Androcentrism in prescriptive grammar: Singular "they", sex-indefinite "he" and "he or she"', *Language in Society* 4, 1975b, pp. 129-46.

Borker, R., 'Anthropology: Social and cultural perspectives', in McConnell-Ginet et al. (1980), 1980, pp. 26−44.

Broverman, I.K., Vogel, S.R., Broverman, D.W., Clarkson, F.E., & Rosenkrantz, P.S., 'Sex role stereotypes: A current appraisal', *Journal of Social Issues* 28(2), 1972, pp. 59−78.

Brown, P., 'How and why are women more polite: Some evidence from a Mayan community,' in McConnell-Ginet et al. (1980), 1980, pp. 111−36.

89

Brown, P., & Levinson, S., 'Universals in language usage: Politeness phenomena', in E.N. Goody (ed.), *Questions and Politeness: Strategies in Social Interaction* (Cambridge University Press, Cambridge, 1978), pp. 56–324.

Brown, R., & Ford, M., 'Address in American English', in D. Hymes (ed.), *Language in Culture and Society* (Harper and Row, New York, 1964), pp. 234–44.

Brown, R., & Gilman, A., 'The pronouns of power and solidarity', in T.A. Sebeok (ed.), *Style in Language* (MIT Press, Cambridge, Massachusetts, 1960), pp. 253–76. Reprinted in P.P. Giglioli (ed.), *Language and Social Context* (Penguin, Harmondsworth, 1972), pp. 252–82.)

Cass, B., Dawson, M., Temple, D., Wills, S., & Winkler, A., *Why So Few? Women Academics in Australian Universities* (Sydney University Press, Sydney, 1983).

Cherry, L.J., 'Sex differences in child speech: McCarthy revisited', *Research Bulletin* (Educational Testing Service, Princeton, New Jersey, 1975a).

Cherry, L.J., 'Teacher–child verbal interaction: An approach to the study of sex differences', in Thorne & Henley (1975b), 1975b, pp. 172–83.

Christie, F., 'Some current issues in first language writing development', in H. Nicholas (ed.), *Current Issues in Children's Language Development* (Applied Linguistics Association of Australia, Melbourne, 1985a).

Christie, F., 'Young children's writing development: The relationship of written genres to curriculum genres', in B. Bartlett (ed.), *Language in Education* (Brisbane College of Advanced Education, Brisbane, 1985b).

Christie, F., 'Language and schooling', in S. Tchudi (ed.), *Language, Schooling and Society* (Boynton/Cook, Montclair, New Jersey, 1985c).

Condry, J., & Condry, S., 'Sex differences: A study of the eye of the beholder', *Child Development* **47**, 1976, pp. 812–19.

Conklin, N.F., 'Toward a feminist analysis of linguistic behaviour', *University of Michigan Papers in Women's Studies* **1**, 1974, pp. 51–73.

Culler, J., *On Deconstruction: Theory and Criticism after Structuralism* (Routledge & Kegan Paul, London, 1983).

Dubois, B.L., & Crouch, I., 'The question of tag questions in women's speech: They don't really use them, do they?', *Language in Society* **4**, 1976, pp. 289–94.

Eakins, B.W., & Eakins, R.G., *Sex Differences in Human Communication* (Houghton Mifflin, Boston, 1978).

Edelsky, C., 'Acquisition of an aspect of communicative competence: Learning what it means to talk like a lady', in S. Ervin-Tripp & C. Mitchell-Kernan (eds), *Child Discourse* (Academic Press, New York, 1977, pp. 225-43).

Edgar, P., Edgar, D., Poole, M., Roper, T., & Higgs, M., *Under 5 in Australia* (Heinemann, Melbourne, 1973).

Ehrenreich, B., *The Hearts of Men: American Dreams and the Flight from Commitment* (Pluto Press, London, 1983).

Eisenstein, H., *Contemporary Feminist Thought* (Unwin Paperbacks, London, 1984).

Elliot, J., 'Sex role constraints on freedom of discussion: A neglected reality of the classroom', *New Era* **55/56**, 1974 (Reprinted as 'Sex roles and silence in the classroom' in *Spare Rib* **27**.)

Ellmann, M., *Thinking About Women* (Virago, London, 1979).

Faust, B., *Women, Sex and Pornography* (Penguin Australia, Ringwood, Victoria, 1980).

Fichtelius, A., Johansson, I., & Nordin, K., 'Three investigations of sex-associated speech variation in day school', in Kramarae (1980), 1980, pp. 219–25.

Firestone, S., *The Dialectic of Sex: The Case for Feminist Revolution* (Paladin, London, 1972).

Fishman, P.M., 'Interaction: The work women do', *Social Problems* **25**, 1978, pp. 397–416. (Reprinted in Thorne et al. (1983), pp. 89–101.)

Fowler, H.W., *A Dictionary of Modern English Usage*, 2nd edn, rev., Sir Ernest Gowers (Clarendon Press, Oxford, 1965).

Fowler, R., Hodge, B., Kress, G., & Trew, T., *Language and Control* (Routledge & Kegan Paul, London, 1979).

Friedan, B., *The Feminine Mystique* (Penguin, Harmondsworth, 1965).

Gleason, J.B., 'Code switching in children's language', in T. Moore (ed.), *Cognitive Development and the Acquisition of Language* (Academic Press, New York, 1973, pp. 159–67).

Goffman, E., *Gender Advertisements*,(Harper & Row, New York, 1976).

Goldberg, P., 'Are women prejudiced against women?', in Stacey et al. (1974), 1968/1974, pp. 37–42.

Graham, A., 'The making of a non-sexist dictionary', in Thorne & Henley (1975b), 1975, pp. 57–63.

Greer, G., *The Female Eunuch* (Granada, London, 1971).

Guy, G.R., Horvath, B.M., Vonwiller, J., Daisley, E., & Rogers, I., Question intonation in declarative clauses in Australian English: A quantitative study.' Paper presented at the Annual Meeting of the Australian Linguistic Society (Australian National University, 1982).

Guy, G.R., & Vonwiller, J., 'The meaning of an intonation in Australian English', *Australian Journal of Linguistics* **4**(1), 1984, pp. 1–17.

Haas, A., 'Male and female spoken language differences: Stereotypes and evidence', *Psychological Bulletin* **86**(3), 1979, pp. 616–26.

Halliday, M.A.K., 'Anti-languages', *American Anthropologist* **78**(3), 1976, pp. 570–84. (Reprinted in Halliday (1978), pp. 164–82.)

Halliday, M.A.K., *Aims and Perspectives in Linguistics* Occasional Papers, no.1 (Applied Linguistics Association of Australia, Melbourne, 1977).

Halliday, M.A.K., *Language As Social Semiotic: The Social Interpretation of Language and Meaning*, Edward Arnold, London, 1978).

Halliday, M.A.K., 'Language as code and language as behaviour', in R. P. Fawcett, M.A.K. Halliday, S.M. Lamb & A. Makkai (eds.), *The Semiotics of Culture and Language*, vol.1 *Language as Social Semiotic* (Frances Pinter, London, 1984, pp. 3–35).

Halliday, M.A.K., *An Introduction to Functional Grammar* (Edward Arnold, London, 1985).

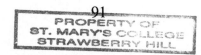

Halliday, M.A.K., & Hasan, R., *Language, Context, and Text: Aspects of language in a social-semiotic perspective* (Oxford University Press, Oxford, 1989).

Hasan, R., 'Text in the systemic-functional model', in W. Dressler (ed.), *Current Trends in Textlinguistics* (Walter de Gruyter, Berlin and New York, 1978, pp. 228–46).

Hasan, R., 'On the notion of text', in J.S. Petofi (ed.), *Text vs. Sentence: Basic Questions of Textlinguistics,* Papers in Textlinguistics, **20**(2) (Hamburg, Buske, 1979, pp. 369–90).

Hasan, R., 'The ontogenesis of ideology: An interpretation of mother child talk', in T. Threadgold et al. (1986, pp. 125–46.

Heath, S.B., *Ways with Words: Language, Life, and Work in Communities and Classrooms* (Cambridge University Press, Cambridge, 1983).

Hellinger, M., '"For men must work and women must weep": Sexism in English language textbooks used in German schools', in Kramarae (1980), 1980, pp. 267–75.

Henley, N., *Body Politics: Power, Sex and Nonverbal Communication* (Prentice-Hall, Englewood Cliffs, New Jersey, 1977).

Hopper, R., Knapp, M.L., & Scott, L., 'Couples' personal idioms: Exploring intimate talk', *Journal of Communication* **31**, 1981, pp. 23–33.

Horvath, B.M., *Variation in Australian English: The Sociolects of Sydney* (Cambridge University Press, Cambridge, 1985).

Janssen-Jurreit, M., 'The dialectic of man and woman', in *Sexism: The Male Monopoly of History and Thought* (Pluto Press, London, 1982, pp. 299–307).

Jespersen, O., *Language: Its Nature, Development and Origin* (Allen & Unwin, London, 1922).

Keesing, N., *Lily on the Dustbin: Slang of Australian Women and Families* (Penguin Australia, Ringwood, Victoria, 1982).

Ker, M., *Pacific Aphrodite* (Mills & Boon, London, 1984).

Key, M.R., *Male/Female Language* (Scarecrow Press, Metuchen, New Jersey, 1975).

Kramarae, C. (ed.), *The Voices and Words of Women and Men*, Special issue of *Women's Studies International Quarterly* **3**(2/3), 1980.

Kramer, C., 'Sex-related differences in address systems', *Anthropological Linguistics* **17**(5), 1975, pp. 198–210.

Kramer, C., Thorne, B., & Henley, N., 'Review essay: Perspectives on language and communication', *Signs: Journal of Women in Culture and Society* **3**, 1978, pp. 638–51.

Kress, G., & Hodge, R., *Language as Ideology* (Routledge & Kegan Paul, London, 1979).

Kroch, A.S., 'Toward a theory of social dialect variation', *Language in Society* **7**, 1978, pp. 17–36.

Labov, W., 'Rules for ritual insults', in *Language in the Inner City: Studies in the Black English Vernacular* (University of Pennsylvania Press, Philadelphia, 1972a), pp. 297–353.

Labov, W., *Sociolinguistic Patterns* (University of Pennsylvania Press, Philadelphia, 1972b).

Lakoff, R., 'Language and woman's place', *Language in Society* **2**, 1973, pp. 45–79.

Lakoff, R., *Language and Woman's Place* (Harper & Row, New York, 1975). Incorporates Lakoff, 1973.

Lakoff, R., 'Stylistic strategies within a grammar of style', in Orasanu et al. (1979), 1979, pp. 53–78.

Langer, E., 'The women of the telephone company', *New York Review of Books* **14**, 1970, 12 & 26 March.

Le Carré, J., *Call for the Dead* (Penguin, Harmondsworth, 1964).

Legman, G., *Rationale of the Dirty Joke: An Analysis of Sexual Humor*, 2 vols (Granada, London, 1972).

Lewis, M., 'Parents and children: Sex-role development', *School Review* **80**, 1972, pp. 229–40.

Lewis, M., & Freedle, R., 'Mother-infant dyad: The cradle of meaning', in P. Pliner, L. Krames & T. Alloyway (eds.), *Communication and Affect, Language and Thought* (Academic Press, New York, 1973).

Lieberman, P., *Intonation, Perception and Language* (MIT Press, Cambridge, Massachusetts, 1967).

McCarthy, D., 'Some possible explanations of sex differences in language development and disorders', *Journal of Psychology* **35**, 1953, pp. 155–60.

McConnell-Ginet, S., 'Intonation in a man's world', *Signs: Journal of Women in Culture and Society* **3**, 1978a, pp. 541–59.

McConnell-Ginet, S., 'Address forms in sexual politics', in D. Butturff & E.L. Epstein (eds), *Women's Language and Style* (University of Akron Press, Akron, 1978b, pp. 23–35.

McConnell-Ginet, S., 'Prototypes, pronouns and persons', in Mathiot (1979), 1979, pp. 63–83.

McConnell-Ginet, S., 'Linguistics and the feminist challenge', in McConnell-Ginet et al. (1980), 1980, pp. 3–25.

McConnell-Ginet, S., Review article in *Language* **59**, 1983, pp. 373–91. (Reviews of Orasanu et al. (1979) and Vetterling-Braggin (1981).)

McConnell-Ginet, S., Borker, R., & Furman, N. (eds.), *Women and Language in Literature and Society* (Praeger, New York, 1980).

MacCormack, C., & Strathern, M. (eds.), *Nature, Culture and Gender* (Cambridge University Press, Cambridge, 1980).

MacKay, D.G., & Konishi, T., 'Personification and the pronoun problem', in Kramarae (1980), 1980, pp. 149–63.

The Macquarie Dictionary, ed. A. Delbridge (Macquarie Library, St Leonard's, NSW, 1981).

Mainardi, P., 'Quilts: The great American art', *Radical America* **7**(1), 1973, pp. 36–68.

Maltz, D.N., & Borker, R.A., 'A cultural approach to male-female miscommunication', in J. J. Gumperz (ed.), *Language and Social Identity* (Cambridge University Press, Cambridge, 1982, pp. 196–216.

Martin, J.R., 'Language, register and genre', in *Children Writing: Reader* (ECT418 Language Studies), Deakin University, Geelong, Victoria, 1984, pp. 21–30.

Martin, J.R., 'Types of writing in infants' and primary school', in L. Unsworth (ed.), *Proceedings of Macarthur Institute of Higher Education Reading/Language Symposium 5: Reading, Writing and Spelling*, 1985a, pp. 34–55.

Martin, J.R., 'Process and text: Two aspects of human semiosis', in J.D. Benson & W.S. Greaves (eds.), *Systemic Perspectives on Discourse, Volume 1: Selected Theoretical Papers from the Ninth International Systemic Workshop* (Ablex, Norwood, New Jersey, 1985b), pp. 248–74.

Martin, J.R., 'Lexical cohesion, field and genre: Parcelling experience and discourse goals', in J.E. Copeland (ed.), *Text Semantics and Discourse Semantics, Proceedings of the Second Rice Symposium in Linguistics and Semiotics*, forthcoming).

Martin, J.R., 'Grammaticalising ecology: The politics of baby seals and kangaroos', in T. Threadgold et al. (1986), pp. 225–67.

Martin, J.R., 'Grammatical conspiracies in Tagalog: Family, face and fate—with regard to Benjamin Lee Whorf', in J.D. Benson, M.J. Cummings, & W.S. Greaves (eds.), *Linguistics in a Systemic Perspective* (Benjamins, Amsterdam, 1988).

Martin, J.R., *Factual Writing: exploring and challenging social reality* (Oxford University Press, Oxford, 1989).

Martin, J.R., & Rothery, J., *Writing Project Report 1980: Working Papers in Linguistics 1* (University of Sydney, 1980).

Martin, J.R., & Rothery, J., *Writing Project Report 1981. Working Papers in Linguistics 2* (University of Sydney, 1981).

Martin, J.R., & Rothery, J., 'Choice of genre in a suburban primary school'. Paper presented at Annual Conference of the Applied Linguistics Association of Australia (Alice Springs, NT, 1984).

Mathiot, M., assisted by Roberts, M., 'Sex roles as revealed through referential gender in American English', in Mathiot (1979), 1979, pp. 1–47.

Mathiot, M. (ed.), *Ethnolinguistics: Boas, Sapir and Whorf Revisited*, Contributions to the Sociology of Language 27, (Mouton, The Hague, 1979).

Miller, C., & Swift, K., *Words and Women* (Doubleday, New York, 1977).

Miller, C., & Swift, K., *The Handbook of Non-Sexist Writing for Writers, Editors and Speakers* (Women's Press, London, 1981). (British Edition revised by Stephanie Dowrick, 1979).

Millett, K., *Sexual Politics* (Avon, New York, 1971).

Mitchell, A.G., & Delbridge, A., *The Speech of Australian Adolescents* (Angus & Robertson, Sydney, 1965).

Mitchell, J., *Women's Estate* (Penguin, Harmondsworth, 1971).

Murnane, G., *Tamarisk Row* (Angus & Robertson, Sydney, 1979).

The National Times—Women's Role (Allen & Unwin, Sydney, 1983).

Nichols, P., 'Women in their speech communities', in McConnell-Ginet et al. (1980), 1980, pp. 140–9.

Oakley, A., *Sex, Gender and Society* (Sun Books, Melbourne, 1972).

O'Barr, W.M., *Linguistic Evidence: Language, Power and Strategy in the Courtroom*, Studies on Law and Social Contract (Academic Press, New York, 1982).

O'Barr, W.M., & Atkins, B.K., '"Women's language" or "powerless language"?', in McConnell-Ginet et al. (1980), 1980, pp. 93–110.

Orasanu, J., Slater, M.K., & Adler, L.L. (eds.), 'Language, Sex and Gender: Does "La Différence" Make a Difference?' *Annals of the New York Academy of Sciences* 327, 1979.

Ordoubadian, R., 'Sexism and language structure', in W. Wölck & P.L. Garvin (eds.), *The Fifth LACUS Forum 1978* (Hornbeam Press, Columbia, SC, 1979, pp. 415−21.

Packham, G., A study of questions asked by men and women in the graduate classroom. Unpublished (graduate student) paper (University of Illinois at Chicago Circle, 1982).

Parker, A.M., *Sex Differences in Classroom Intellectual Argumentation* (MS thesis, Pennsylvania State University, 1973).

Parliament of Victoria, Legal and Constitutional Committee, *Report on Interpretation Bill 1982* (Melbourne, 1983).

Peterson, A., 'Mrs, er Miss, er Ms Ferraro's title fight', *Sydney Morning Herald*, 28 August 1984.

Philips, S.U., 'Sex differences and language', *Annual Review of Anthropology* **9**, 1980, pp. 523−44.

Plum, G., 'Field in contextual theory: A proposal for its systemic representation'. (Department of Linguistics, University of Sydney, mimeo, 1984).

Poynton, C., 'Terms of address as markers of social relations in Australian English'. (Department of Linguistics, University of Sydney, mimeo, 1981).

Poynton, C., 'The linguistic realisation of social relations: Terms of address in Australian English', *Collected Papers on Normal Aspects of Speech and Language, 52nd ANZAAS Conference* (Speech and Language Research Centre, Occasional Papers, Macquarie University, North Ryde, NSW, 1982), pp. 253−69.

Poynton, C., 'Names as vocatives: forms and functions', *Nottingham Linguistic Circular*, **13**, 1984, pp. 1−34.

Poynton, C., *Address and the Semiotics of Social Relations*, PhD thesis (Department of Linguistics, University of Sydney, in preparation).

Rich, A., *On Lies, Secrets and Silence: Selected Prose 1966−1978* (Norton, New York, 1979).

Roberts, B., 'Ockers and malespeak: Why men and women don't speak the same language in Australia', *Australian Society* **3**(8), 1984, pp. 13−16.

Roget's Thesaurus of English Words and Phrases, ed. R.A. Dutch (Longman, London, 1962).

Roget's Thesaurus of English Words and Phrases, ed. S.M. Lloyd (Longman, Harlow, Essex, 1982).

Rothery, J., 'Narrative: Vicarious experience', in J.R. Martin & J. Rothery, *Writing Report 1980. Working Papers in Linguistics 1* (University of Sydney, Sydney, 1980).

Rothery, J., 'The development of genres—primary to junior secondary school', in *Children Writing: Study Guide*, ECT418 Language Studies (Deakin University, Geelong, Victoria, 1984), pp. 67−114.

Rothery, J., *The Linguistic Realisation of Narrative Writing by Year Six Children*, PhD thesis (working title) (Department of Linguistics, University of Sydney, in preparation).

Rudes, B., & Healy, B., 'Is she for real?: The concepts of femaleness and maleness in the gay world', in Mathiot (1979), 1979, pp. 49−61.

Sachs, J., 'Cues to the identification of sex in children's speech', in Thorne & Henley (1975b), 1975, pp. 152−71.

Salem, J.C., 'On naming the oppressor: What Woolf avoids saying in *A Room of One's Own*', in Kramarae (1980), 1980, pp. 209–18.

Sarah, E., 'Teachers and students in the classroom: An examination of classroom interaction', in Spender & Sarah (1980), 1980, pp. 155–64.

Schneider, J.W., & Hacker, S.L., 'Sex role imagery and the use of the generic 'man' in introductory texts', *American Sociologist* **8**, 1973, pp. 12–18.

Schulz, M.R., 'The semantic derogation of women', in Thorne & Henley (1975b), 1975, pp. 64–75.

Sears, P.S., & Feldman, D.H., 'Teacher interactions with boys and with girls', in Stacey et al. (1974), 1966/1974, pp. 147–58.

The Shorter Oxford English Dictionary on Historical Principles, 3rd edn (with addenda), ed. C.T. Onions (Clarendon Press, Oxford, 1973).

Shuster, J., Grammatical forms marked for male and female in English. Unpublished (graduate student) paper (Department of Anthropology, University of Chicago, 1973).

Shuster, J., Verb forms of 'power and solidarity': sex as the basis of power. Unpublished paper (University of Chicago, 1974).

Silveira, J., 'Generic masculine words and thinking', in Kramarae (1980), 1980, pp. 165–78.

Smith, D.M., 'Language, speech and ideology: A conceptual framework', in R.W. Shuy & R.W. Fasold (eds.), *Language Attitudes: Current Trends and Prospects* (Georgetown University Press, Washington, DC, 1973), pp. 97–112.

Smith, P.M., 'Sex markers in speech', in K.R. Scherer & H. Giles (eds.), *Social Markers in Speech* (Cambridge University Press, Cambridge, 1979), pp. 109–46.

Spender, D., 'Talking in class', in Spender & Sarah (1980), 1980a, pp. 148–54.

Spender, D., *Man Made Language* (Routledge & Kegan Paul, London, 1980b).

Spender, D., *Women of Ideas (And What Men Have Done to Them): From Aphra Behn to Adrienne Rich* (Routledge & Kegan Paul, London, 1982).

Spender, D., & Sarah, E. (eds.), *Learning to Lose: Sexism and Education* (Women's Press, London, 1980).

Stacey, J., Béreaud, S., & Daniels, J. (eds.), *And Jill Came Tumbling After: Sexism in American Education* (Dell, New York, 1974).

Stanley, J.P., 'Paradigmatic woman: The prostitute', in D.L. Shores & C.P. Hines (eds.) , *Papers in Language Variation* (University of Alabama Press, Alabama, 1974), pp. 303–21.

Steedman, C., *The Tidy House: Little Girls Writing* (Virago, London, 1982).

Thoman, E.B., Leiderman, P.H., & Olson, J.P., 'Neonate-mother interaction during breast feeding', *Developmental Psychology* **6**, 1972, pp. 110–18.

Thorne, B., & Henley, N., 'Difference and dominance: An overview', in Thorne & Henley (1975b), 1975a, pp. 5–42.

Thorne, B., & Henley, N. (eds.), *Language and Sex: Difference and Dominance* (Newbury House, Rowley, Massachusetts, 1975b).

Thorne, B., Kramarae, C., & Henley, N. (eds.), *Language, Gender and Society* (Newbury House, Rowley, Massachusetts, 1983).

Threadgold, T., Grosz, E. A., Kress, G., & Halliday, M.A.K. (eds.), *Semiotics, Ideology, Language* (Sydney Association for Studies in Society and Culture, Sydney, 1986).

Thwaite, A., *Sexism in Three Mills & Boon Romances*, BA Honours thesis (Department of Linguistics, University of Sydney, 1983).

Ventola, E., 'The structure of casual conversation in English', *Journal of Pragmatics* **3**, 1979, pp. 267—98.

Ventola, E., 'Contrasting schematic structures in service encounters', *Applied Linguistics* **4**(3), 1983, pp. 242—58.

Ventola, E., *The Structure of Social Interaction: a systemic approach to the semiotics of service encounters* (Frances Pinter, London, 1987).

Vetterling-Braggin, M. (ed.), *Sexist Language: A Modern Philosophical Analysis* (Littlefield Adams, Totowa, New Jersey, 1981).

Ward, R., *The Australian Legend* (Oxford University Press, Melbourne, 1958).

Wearing, B., *The Ideology of Motherhood: A Study of Sydney Suburban Mothers*, Studies in Society 21 (Allen & Unwin, Sydney, 1984).

Wescott, R.W., 'The phonology and morphology of American English slang', in *Sound and Sense: Linguistic Essays on Phonosemic Subjects* (Jupiter Press, Lake Bluff, Illinois, 1976/1980), pp. 394—405.

West, C., 'Against our will: Male interruptions of females in cross-sex conversation', in Orasanu et al. (1979), 1979, pp. 81—97.

West, C., & Zimmerman, D., 'Women's place in everyday talk: Reflections on parent-child interaction', *Social Problems* **24**, 1977, pp. 521—9.

Whorf, B.L., *Language, Thought and Reality: Selected Writings of Benjamin Lee Whorf*, edited and introduced by J.B. Carroll (MIT Press, Cambridge, Massachusetts, 1956).

Williams, J.E., & Bennett, S.M., 'The definition of sex stereotypes via the adjective check list', *Sex Roles* **1**, 1975, pp. 327—37.

Wolfson, N., & Manes, J., 'Don't "dear" me!', in McConnell-Ginet et al. (1980), 1980, pp. 79—92.

Zimmerman, D., & West, C., 'Sex roles, interruptions and silences in conversation', in Thorne & Henley (1975b), 1975, pp. 105—29.

Further reading

Introductions, overviews, collections of papers

Eakins, B,W., & Eakins, R.G., *Sex Differences in Human Communication* (Houghton Mifflin, Boston, 1978).

Useful introductory course book, from a Communications rather than a Linguistics perspective. Summarises much of the relevant research in very accessible style. Covers non-verbal as well as verbal communication.

Key, M.R., *Male/Female Language* (Scarecrow Press, Metuchen, New Jersey, 1975).

Somewhere in between a coursebook and a general book. Covers a wide range of topics in a very accessible style.

Kramarae, C., *Women and Men Speaking: Frameworks for Analysis* (Newbury House, Rowley, Massachusetts, 1981).

Presents and discusses four analytical approaches to language and gender, in varying degrees of detail. Adds a further sociological/social psychological dimension to the approach adopted here.

Kramarae, C., (ed.), *The Voices and Words of Women and Men*, Special issue of *Women's Studies International Quarterly*, vol. 3, no.2/3, 1980.

An excellent collection, covering a wide range of topics including adult–child interaction at home and school, sexism in English language textbooks, and a fascinating paper on personification in children's literature.

Lakoff, R., *Language and Woman's Place* (Harper & Row, New York, 1975).

Problematic in many respects, since she uses introspection as her only source of data—a course fraught with peril in ideologically sensitive areas and liable not to reveal all that might be revealed by systematic and rigorous analysis of actual data. Indispensable reading, nevertheless: she started numerous fascinating hares (many of which are still up and running in the literature) and her work is constantly referred to and forms the starting-point for much research.

McConnell-Ginet, S., Borker, R. & Furman, N., (eds.), *Women and Language in Literature and Society* (Praeger, New York, 1980).

An exceedingly well-organised collection, beginning with a set of overview essays from different disciplinary perspectives (linguistics, anthropology, literary theory) followed by a section devoted to each area.

Miller, C., & Swift, K., *Words and Women* (Anchor Press/Doubleday, New York, 1977). It has also been published more recently by Penguin.

Designed for the general public, written by two freelance writers, this is a delightful introduction full of good sense and fascinating detail.

Spender, D., *Man Made Language* (Routledge & Kegan Paul, London, 1980).

Based on empirical work that is unfortunately not presented in detail. Spender knows the issues, and she writes extremely well—no impersonal academic style either, but the voice of an articulate and informed feminist who gives you the ideology and its consequences right between the eyes.

Thorne, B., & Henley, N., (eds.), *Language and Sex: Difference and Dominance* (Newbury House, Rowley, Massachusetts, 1975).

The first comprehensive collection of papers in the area, many of them key papers still. Thorne & Henley's introductory overview paper is a classic and their annotated bibliography, organised into sections according to topic and cross-referenced, was for many years an indispensable tool. It has now been superseded by the up-dated version in Thorne et al. (1983).

Thorne, B., Kramarae, C., & Henley, N., (eds.), *Language, Gender and Society* (Newbury House, Rowley, Massachusetts, 1983).

A follow-up to the previous volume. Consists of an introductory overview by the editors, nine selected papers on a wide range of topics (several dealing specifically with men's speech), and an extensive annotated bibliography, updated from Thorne & Henley's (1975) bibliography. Several of the papers are reprinted from less readily available sources and the bibliography is an indispensable resource.

Vetterling-Braggin, M., (ed.), *Sexist Language: A Modern Philosophical Analysis* (Littlefield Adams, Totowa, New Jersey, 1981).

Some of the papers in the first section are perhaps a little too philosophical for some tastes, but subsequent sections cover a range of topics. A particularly good feature is that many of the papers are discussed or replied to by other writers, so one has the sense of an ongoing dialogue.

Women and Language News (current editors: Cheris Kramarae and Paula Treichler, University of Illinois at Urbana-Champaign.)

The latest information on research, conferences, debates, publications. Takes up issues concerning language and gender, particularly as they affect women, in all areas of life. The Spring 1984 issue, for instance, has several articles and an annotated bibliography on women, medicine and language.

For information about subscriptions contact:

Karen Lee Cole
Women and Language News
Centenary College of Louisiana
2911 Centenary Blvd
Shreveport LA 71104 USA

Education

Spender, D., & Sarah, E., (eds.), *Learning to Lose: Sexism and Education* (Women's Press, London, 1980).

    Contains a number of papers directly (and indirectly) concerned with language. Jackson's paper on sex education for girls raises a plethora of ideologically sensitive issues involving field and genre and it alone is worth getting hold of this collection for. Spender's and Sarah's contributions on classroom talk are stimulating and informative.

Stacey, J., Béreaud, S., & Daniels, J., (eds.), *And Jill Came Tumbling After: Sexism in American Education* (Dell, New York, 1974).

    A collection that casts its net well back behind the early 1970s to include some classic older papers (including the Sears & Feldman paper referred to in the text), as well as scholarly papers and more personal comments from individuals involved in all levels of education from elementary to tertiary.

Stanworth, M., *Gender and Schooling: A Study of Sexual Divisions in the Classroom* (Hutchinson in association with the Explorations in Feminism Collective, London, 1983).

    Reports a study revealing how the day-to-day management of classes marginalises girls. Very sobering, even for experienced teachers. One of the best things I've read in this area, and it's short.

Reading and Writing

Gallagher, K., & Peery, A., (compilers), *Bibliography of Materials on Sexism and Sex-Role Stereotyping in Children's Books* (Lollipop Power, Chapel Hill, North Carolina). (Revised annually.)

    Abstracts, some with comments, of articles, curriculum materials, and non-sexist bibliographies culled from the professional journal literature. Mainly, but not exclusively, American material.

Russ, J., *How to Suppress Women's Writing* (University of Texas Press, Austin, 1983). (British edition published by Women's Press, London, 1984.)

    All the techniques that have been used—and still are being used, in many cases—to discourage women from writing and to tell them that what they've written is no good/not good enough/good but not what was wanted/really written by someone else . . . Russ herself says that

100

what she has done is not to provide a history but 'a sketch of an analytic tool: patterns in the suppression of women's writing'. Covers all sorts of writing, not just fiction.

Showalter, E., *A Literature of Their Own: British Women Novelists from Brontë to Lessing*, rev. edn (Virago, London, 1982).

From the blurb: 'Using history and sociology, this account of the female tradition and its social and literary history . . . show[s] how the growth of female consciousness helped shape the novel'. As well as the text, it contains both an extensive bibliography and a biographical index of women novelists.

Steedman, C., *The Tidy House: Little Girls Writing* (Virago, London, 1982).

An absorbing analysis of the role of writing for the three authors of the story called 'The Tidy House', in coming to terms with being female in their particular world. Steedman speaks of their using the writing in the process of being 'agents of their own socialization'. She sets the issue of little girls writing in a historical context and investigates Victorian and contemporary conceptions of self as seen through speech and writing.

Stinton, J., (ed.), *Racism and Sexism in Children's Books*, rev. edn (Writers and Readers Publishing Cooperative, London, 1979).

A collection of articles with an overview essay. Less polemical than some other publications in this area and deals with the more popular things kids read, not just what teachers give them in school.

Non-verbal communication

Goffman, E., *Gender Advertisements* (Harper & Row, New York, 1976).
A look at how the female body is used in advertising—illustrated.

Henley, N., *Body Politics: Power, Sex and Nonverbal Communication* (Prentice-Hall, Englewood Cliffs, New Jersey, 1977).

Looks at all the various ways in which humans use their bodies in the relentless conflict between male and female. Written in a very approachable style—high school students would enjoy it, but it is not a textbook as such.

Counter-sexist guidelines

Blaubergs, M., 'An analysis of classic arguments against changing sexist language', in C. Kramarae (ed.), *The Voices and Words of Women and Men*, Special issue of *Women's Studies International Quarterly*, vol. 3, no.2/3, 1980, pp. 135–47.

Counters eight classic types of argument, ranging from the 'why should we bother?' through the 'why can't I say what I like?' to arguments based on 'real meaning' and authority in language use. The bibliography includes references to various counter-sexist guidelines adopted by publishers and other organisations.

Miller, C., & Swift, K., *The Handbook of Non-Sexist Writing for Writers, Editors and Speakers* (Women's Press, London, 1981). (British edition revised by Stephanie Dowrick.)

Comprehensive within the limits of an almost exclusive focus on lexis; sensible and feasible suggestions, well-organised.

Technical terms

Acknowledgements

Grateful acknowledgement is made to the following sources for material used in this book.

pp.13, extracts from J. Condry & S. Condry, 'Sex differences', *Child Development*, vol.47, pp.812–19. © The Society for Research in Child Development, Inc. Reprinted by permission.

pp.13, 17, extracts from G. Kress & R. Hodge, *Language as Ideology* (Routledge & Kegan Paul, London, 1979). Reprinted by permission of the authors.

p.14, extract: Reprinted from Peter L. Berger and Thomas Luckmann, *The social construction of reality* (Penguin Books, Ltd. 1967) Copyright © Peter L. Berger and Thomas Luckmann, 1966. By permission of Penguin Books, Ltd. and Doubleday & Co., Inc.

p.16, Table 1.1: from G. Kress & R. Hodge, *Language as Ideology* (Routledge & Kegan Paul, London, 1979). Reprinted by permission of the authors.

pp.29, 31, 32, extracts from P.S. Sears & D.H. Feldman, 'Teacher interactions with boys and with girls', in J. Stacey, S. Bereaud & J. Daniels (eds.), *And Jill Came Tumbling After* (Dell, New York, 1974).

pp.32–34, 38, 67, extracts from D. Spender, 'Talking in class', in D. Spender & E. Sarah (eds), *Learning to Lose* (Women's Press, London, 1980). Reprinted by permission of the author.

pp.45–50, extracts from C. Kramer, B. Thorne & N. Henley, 'Review essay: Perspectives on language and communication', *Signs*, vol. 3, pp. 638–51. © 1978 by the University of Chicago Press. Reprinted by permission of the publisher.

pp.46, 47, extracts from M. Mathiot assisted by M. Roberts, 'Sex roles as revealed through referential gender in American English', in M. Mathiot (ed.), *Ethnolinguistics: Boas, Sapir, and Whorf* (Mouton, The Hague, 1979). Reprinted by permission of the publisher.

pp.47–8, Tables 3.1 and 3.2: from M. Mathiot assisted by M. Roberts, 'Sex roles as revealed through referential gender in American English' in M. Mathiot (ed.), *Ethnolinguistics: Boas, Sapir, and Whorf* (Mouton, The Hague, 1979). Reprinted by permission of the publisher.

p.60, Tables 4.1 and 4.2: from J. Archer & B. Lloyd, *Sex and Gender* (Penguin Books, Harmondsworth, 1982); based on Williams and Bennett (1975). Reprinted by permission of Penguin Books, Ltd. and the authors.

p.70, Table 5.1: from C. Edelsky, 'Acquisition of an aspect of communicative competence', in S. Ervin-Tripp & C. Mitchell-Kernan (eds.), *Child Discourse* (Academic Press, New York, 1977). Reprinted by permission of the publisher and the author.

p.74, Figure 5.1: from J.R. Martin, 'Process and text', in J.D. Benson & W.S. Greaves (eds.), *Systemic Perspectives on Discourse* (Ablex, Norwood, NJ, 1985). Reprinted by permission of the author.

104

3Ms

This book is to be returned on or before

**Books are to be returned on or before
the last date below.**

1 99

- 7 JUN 1999   - 8 MAY 2002

25 OCT 1999   - 6 JAN 2003

- 2 OCT 2000   1 7 MAR 2003

- 2 APR 2001

- 8 APR 2002

LIBREX —

POYNTON, Cate

182132   10 MAR 1999   1 6 NOV 1998   2 0 APR 1998
                        1 0 NOV 1998

28 APR 1999